How to Walk a Dog

How to Walk a Dog

MIKE WHITE

ILLUSTRATIONS BY SHARON MURDOCH

ALLEN&UNWIN
SYDNEY·MELBOURNE·AUCKLAND·LONDON

First published in 2019

Text © Mike White, 2019
Illustrations © Sharon Murdoch, 2019

Allen & Unwin
Level 3, 228 Queen Street
Auckland 1010, New Zealand
Phone: (64 9) 377 3800
Email: info@allenandunwin.com
Web: www.allenandunwin.co.nz

83 Alexander Street
Crows Nest NSW 2065, Australia
Phone: (61 2) 8425 0100

A catalogue record for this book is available from the National Library
of New Zealand.

ISBN 978 1 98854 720 6

Design by Kate Barraclough
Set in 11.5pt/17pt Adobe Caslon Pro
Printed in Australia by McPherson's Printing Group
3 5 7 9 10 8 6 4 2

To Nik. Haven't we been the luckiest.

Contents

Introduction

E ach morning, I close our front door, clip the lead on to Cooper's collar, restrain his enthusiasm as he weaves through the gate and jumps into the back of the car, and then we set off for the dog park. It's a five-minute drive, and on the way we drop off my partner, Nikki, so she can walk down to her work in the city. When we arrive at the dog park, Cooper leaps out as soon as the car's hatch is open a crack, and flies down the path. By the time I've selected a stick from the bundle I keep in the car, he is ready below me, waiting for the first throw. And thus the day's excitement truly begins for him.

Our dog park is down a small side road, surrounded by bush, narrow at both ends and bulbous in the middle— the shape of a python that's swallowed a wallaby. At the top, under high-voltage power lines that hiss and sizzle in the rain, is a carpark where council workers eat pies for lunch, tradesmen snooze and hoons pull doughnuts on weekends.

At the other end is a community garden, one of those green spaces where everyone has a small plot of hope. In summer, lettuces and potatoes emerge, unattended courgettes swell to marrows, and the communal compost heap is a pyre of rot irresistible to many of our dogs.

In between the carpark's asphalt and the vegetable garden's seduction are several acres of sloping grass and trees, with some of the loveliest views over Wellington harbour you'll find anywhere in the city. For the past ten years, we've watched this city and seascape in all its shades on a spectrum from blue to bleakest black, from sparkling to malevolent. Those days where the planes taking off from the isthmus between Lyall Bay and Evans Bay seem to just hang in the air, or sunlight shafts through low cloud and illuminates distant Hutt Valley's grey like some godly spotlight.

The park sits between well-heeled and well-desired Brooklyn above and slightly bohemian and very Green Aro Valley below. I've always wondered how such a prime spot so close to the city has avoided being developed, and it seems to be the result of good fortune as much as great foresight. It was once home to a hospital, the foundations of which remain at one edge. Other iterations followed, other plans were made, but eventually the area was deemed part of the town belt, inviolate unless future councillors consider it too valuable to be just the home of courting tūī and romping dogs, as it is now.

It has a small flat level at the top, a giant gum, pine and pōhutukawa placed across it like arboreal statues. From there, the park slides gently down, an easy incline that turns to waterlogged treachery in winter rains. And at one edge is a separate, secret finger of the park, fringed by a reckless mix of blackberries and regenerating native shrubs. At the very end there used to be a kids' rope swing, but the rope frayed long ago and, anyway, the council frowns deeply on such unregulated adventure.

If I stand where the kids used to launch themselves from, and the sun is out, I can tell the season by where my shadow falls each morning, like a rudimentary sundial. At the summer solstice, my outline darkens the trunk of a sickly pine sapling directly in front of me. Deep into June, my shadow lies 90 degrees to my left, in a patch of māhoe (whiteywood) trees. I like the sense of time gently changing despite my daily routine remaining the same.

Dogs like routine. Oh, they love spontaneity, but they rely on routine, expect it, demand it. Cooper, an abandoned farm dog we discovered at the SPCA, knows the routine from the moment our alarm goes off in the morning to the moment our light goes off at night. The day is delineated by a series of good things that he anticipates, relishes and moves on from—to the next good thing. It's a simple existence in a sense, one of rote, which we might think borders on boring. But show me a dog who doesn't enthusiastically eat the same meal it's had for years, or bound along the same walk it always has, tail skyward.

For Cooper, the morning trip to our dog park has been a constant since we first got him. Its attraction never pales. He never understands how it takes me so long to get ready, and counts off every necessity as it's arranged: jacket, gumboots, cap, keys . . . By the time I'm heading to the front door and grabbing his lead from the windowsill, he's already sitting outside on the top step, ready to be clipped on. As soon as he hears the click of the lead's catch, he's leaping down the steps, pulling me towards the car. On our way to the park, he stands silently in the back of the car as we drive from our little home by the sea towards the city, and carefully monitors our route, though it never varies. But from the moment I flick the indicator to turn off the main road and veer down to the park, he starts squealing. It's excitement, expectation, sheer eagerness for what lies immediately ahead—for the dog park, a kind of scruffy suburban Elysian Fields. Only when I've flung the first stick as far as I can and Cooper has sprinted to retrieve it does any sense of calm replace that utter urgency of anticipation.

And so it is, every weekday, every morning, much the same. The mystery of why repetition doesn't reduce a dog's enjoyment of a walk perhaps says more about our own threshold for joy than it does about dogs' dullness.

I've had dogs for much of my life, and have always seen walking them as one of the world's true pleasures. What is it they say about golf? A good walk spoiled? Walking your dog is the opposite—it's a walk infinitely enhanced by your dog's absolute delight. You can't help but share some of it.

I started walking dogs when I was a teenager. My father had just died, my sister had left for university, our previous dog had to be put down, and our family had almost instantly shrunk from five to two. So, when we got a new dog to help make the house feel less empty and our lives more full, the deal was that my mum would walk him in the morning and I'd walk him after school. I would take Gyp, a black-and-white mongrel, to a small park near a maternity hospital, with two ancient oak trees and enough space for him to play and career. This daily task never seemed a chore.

And, years later, I think I still gain as much pleasure as Cooper does from each morning's trip to the dog park. The routine might always be the same, but no day is. The people we meet, the conversations we have, the light across the city, the shadowplay on the harbour—all vary by small degree.

Those of us who gather at our park, whose daily schedules coincide, have over the years become acquainted and close. We're linked by the fundamental fact of owning and exercising a dog, but it's become much more than glancing interaction. As our dogs chase and sniff and stray into the bushes, we stand and chat and laugh. We see each other most days, know much about each other's lives, and have shared more than you'd expect in a public place. Every day I learn a lot. And all in a setting where you're surrounded by dogs suffused with the joy of being outdoors, surrounded by grass and wind and excitement.

It's all so simple, but so happy.

I always think it's the perfect way to start each day.

1.
The names we give them

C ooper. It could have been worse. Quite a lot worse.

As we collected our new dog from the SPCA, we mulled over whether to change the name he'd been allotted while in there and anoint him with something original. Cooper was fine as a name, but calling him something we'd chosen would somehow make him seem more like our dog, rather than someone else's that we'd inherited.

But then, as we waited for the paperwork to be completed in the cramped entrance of Wellington's old SPCA, a staff member came down the stairs, a ginger-and-white puppy curled between her elbow and armpit, and presented it to a couple standing beside us.

'Here's Ladybug!' she sang out excitedly.

The guy, maybe 30, with a short blond haircut and tattoos scattered down his forearms, didn't seem to respond with equal enthusiasm or the delight you'd have hoped for.

Right about then, we figured Cooper was actually a pretty good name for our new pup, and there was no need to change it.

It had a good ring about it, though it was a bit longer than my other dogs' names had been. Somewhere along the line, I'd collected a piece of wisdom that it was best to give your dog a single-syllable name because it was easy for them to learn. Moreover, in moments of crisis, it was quicker to blurt out one syllable to stop your dog rifling through rubbish bags or running onto the road.

As a teenager, I'd had Gyp, named by the children of his previous owner after a dog in a story book. And then there'd been Cas—I can't remember exactly why we called her that, but it just seemed a nice name.

And now Cooper. The word had a few nice associations. The Mini Cooper was a cool car. There was a punk poet I'd loved called John Cooper Clarke. There's a Dunedin ceramicist called Jim Cooper who makes incredible stuff, including wild-looking dogs. And there was that mysterious robber nicknamed D. B. Cooper who hijacked a plane in the States in the seventies, then parachuted into the night with $200,000 of ransom loot, never to be seen again. That case had always fascinated me.

So we decided to stick with Cooper, figuring it could be shortened in emergencies, and figuring he'd got used to it in his two months at the SPCA, waiting for someone to fall for him.

MINI COOPER,
CAR

JOHN COOPER CLARKE,
POET

JIM COOPER,
CERAMICIST

D. B. COOPER,
ROBBER

COOPER, DOG

PICKING A NAME FOR YOUR DOG is a big thing. When inspiration fails, we often fall back on sentimentality, children's whims or something so completely random it smacks of stabbing a finger at a dictionary.

If all those surveys by pet food and insurance companies are correct, the most popular dog name in New Zealand is Bella for a girl, and Charlie if it's a boy. Interestingly, Bella is also the country's favourite name for cats. Also in vogue for dogs are Max, Molly, Poppy, Coco and Ruby. All these names are pretty popular internationally, too. Bella and Charlie are top in the States, but over there you get a few stateside variants—Moose and Hank made it into the top 40 in 2017 and, according to the delightfully named rover.com, Oreo was at 77, Peanut 85 and Chewy 89. But most of the popular dog names are ones you could also name your child—at a pinch, perhaps, in some cases.

At our dog park, I wander down to be greeted by Jess, Katie, Leo, Louis, Lucy, Barney, Rosie, two Harrys, Holly and Doug. Some names are a bit more old-fashioned—Betty, Bonnie, Agatha, Walter. Some hint at internationalism, such as Frida (after Frida Kahlo), Kobe (perhaps the Japanese city, perhaps basketball star Kobe Bryant—owner Jenny isn't sure why the breeder chose it), Herge (in honour of the creator of Tintin) or Toro (bull in Spanish), the muscular black Lab part-owned by Diego, who hails from Argentina.

Then there are the more prosaic, like Hamish. I really

like Hamish for a dog's name. It just seems so unlikely, without affectation or artifice. And, as is so often the case, it seems to fit the dog. Hamish was taken to the SPCA as a puppy after he was found wandering, dragging his right rear leg, which had been broken for some time. He was pretty forlorn and likewise his future, but the vets did a remarkable thing, removing part of his affected hip joint and leaving him to recuperate. As he gradually recovered, he limped along okay at three-quarter pace, but was unbalanced easily and his damaged back leg dangled uselessly, wasting away.

Of course, such an affliction does a dog few favours at the SPCA, which is in many ways an unfortunate beauty contest. Prospective pet owners examine what's on offer and prize cuteness above character, pedigree above practicality. It's a process as cruel as picking schoolyard sports teams, with the gammy and ungainly the last to be wanted. And nobody wanted Hamish. But then along came Barbara.

Earlier that year, Barbara and John's dog Gina had died of cancer, aged twelve. She'd been ill, and one night just took herself outside to lie under her favourite tree, a spot where she'd spent many happy summers twitching and dreaming. That's where they found her in the morning.

To help fill the gap, Barbara would go to the SPCA, walking dogs and fostering those needing extra care. Hamish needed lots of that as he got back on his feet and moving around after his operation, so Barbara and John gave him a temporary home. Eventually, he was well enough to go back to the SPCA, with Barbara hoping an open-minded and generous family would spot him and fall in love with him. But they didn't. Not after a fortnight, not after a month, not after three months.

Barbara continued to visit the SPCA and take Hamish walking, the heavy drop of the bolt on his cage as she returned him marking the sad end of each trip, an exclamation point to Hamish's bleak situation and Barbara's miserable mood.

But, as much as she missed Hamish and as much as she wanted to give him a home, Barbara felt it was still too soon to get another dog, and she knew John didn't want a puppy. It was true—John didn't want a puppy just then, but nor did he relish a moping wife.

One day, after several months of Barbara pining for Hamish, John returned home and sighed, 'I was going to walk Pace [their daughter's dog] and I almost went to the SPCA to pick up Hamish.' And, for the sake of their marriage and Barbara's well-being, he suggested she bring Hamish home for good.

So she did. And so continued Hamish's remarkable recovery.

When I first met Hamish, that back leg was a redundant appendage, trailing piteously. His chest had grown broad, his front legs sustaining the burden of the back leg he'd discounted. But, gradually, the muscles returned, holding the leg in place, and Hamish learned to rely on it again, carrying it only when tired. In time, we didn't even notice it, forgetting he had no hip joint, so normal was his gait. He was a charmer, a survivor. And Hamish seemed just the sort of name he should have.

In the same vein of old-fashioned boys' names was a dog I once met called Owen. His owner said he named him after the street the SPCA was on. Except it wasn't. It was on Mansfield Street; Owen Street ran around the back. But who'd want a dog called Mansfield, other than those making a literary statement?

Owen was a $4,000 Kelpie–Labrador cross. 'That's how much I'm still paying off,' moaned his owner, lamenting the vet bill Owen had run up. Two years old, Owen had leaped out of the car one day and been hit by another vehicle. His front leg was smashed and he'd ended up with a metal plate in his leg, and spent three months recovering in a downstairs room watching TV. After another three months, he was finally able to run at full speed and turn on a ball again. Like Hamish, you would never have known he was an injury case at all—unless you were Owen's owner staring at his bank account.

Then there's Brian, a big German shepherd owned by our friends Mike and Alli. Mike has had a few German shepherds, and this one started out being called Bro but it sort of morphed into Brian. Mike sometimes wishes he'd stuck with Bro, because so many people ask him why his dog's got such a plain bloke's name.

One of the best down-to-earth dog names I've come across was Gary. I heard his owners calling him one day at the dog park, and couldn't help myself approaching them to ask how he'd got that name. 'Oh, it's a long story,' the guy said, with a hint of hesitancy, as if he'd been asked the same question dozens of times. I had time, I told them, so they obliged with the potted version. They used to have a cat called Dave, but he went missing. So they put up posters around the neighbourhood asking anyone who saw Dave to phone them. And one day this guy rang up and said, 'Have you found Gary?' And, in the midst of their anguish at losing Dave, they just thought it was funny and that Gary would be a really good name for their next pet. Because they never did find Dave.

THEN THERE ARE THE NAMES that aren't so literal, names that are utterly personal to the owner. Squirrel got called that because his owner, Chris, had lived in the States for a while and really liked the squirrels he saw when out hiking. Velo's owner is French and likes cycling. Swanson was named after a character in the TV series *Parks and Recreation*. Wicket was a fluffy Ewok from *Star Wars*. My sister's dog is Maverick, the result of her boys' *Top Gun* phase.

A friend has a dog called Fizz. Her daughter wanted to call it Bingo, which wasn't a great choice, if we're honest, but nor was its pedigree name—Heart of Phoenix. Then, one day, they were drinking Phoenix Orange Fizz, and my friend thought, *Aha! Phoenix* . . . And so the dog got called Fizz. Which is a really good name.

When Valentine came to the park, I assumed he was named after the day, that he must have been a romantic February 14 present. But no. His owner, Phil, said he just wanted something a bit noir, something that sounded like it came from an old movie, more cinematic than soppy sentimental.

One day, a new dog bounded across the park followed by its owner, who was calling for Dante to come to heel. 'Dante?' whispered Barbro, our park's longest-standing member, eyebrows rising and eyes widening. It seemed awfully highbrow for a mongrel who looked anything but regally bred. But you're often struck by incongruities, the gap between name and reality. At the park we also have Moose, who is two kilograms of frilly Yorkshire terrier with a pink collar. And Hannibal, a corgi both mild in demeanour and modest in dimension.

Similarly Major, a small something with an attitude that matched his rank if not his actual size. Major was part Jack Russell—the part that was short, yappy and snotty. Like others before him, Major used to get his kicks circling Cooper, trying to herd him, barking till both left the park with their ears ringing. Cooper largely ignored him, and Major made sure never to get closer than Cooper could lunge. The funniest thing was when Major's owner, Penny, realising everyone had got tired of Major's relentless barking, would try to retrieve him. She'd jog across the park, yelling, 'Major Major Major Major!' with the unavoidable echo of *Catch-22*, the book's absurdity matched and exhibited daily at the dog park.

IN *THE DOMINION POST* THEY have a Pet of the Day section, with a photo and caption of someone's beloved ball of fluff or bone-crunching dominator. It's a great display of the dog-naming range, from banality to invention. At one end you'll get yet another chocolate-coloured Lab called Coco—though the owners of Cadbury the Lab had put a fraction more effort into things. And then, a galaxy away, were the spaniels Mystique and Sirius, pictured holding a squeaky bone that looked like a chunk of Martian rock. Then there was Ruby Lulu, which by itself isn't too bizarre as a name. But Ruby Lulu was apparently a pomadoodle, which sounded like a tropical fruit but I suppose was a cross between a Pomeranian and a poodle—and the combined name-and-breed ensemble sounded like a garish cocktail.

And how about the one called Widow? What kind of name is that for a dog? Hardly cheerful, uplifting or even succinct. And what if it was a boy? 'Here, Widower . . .'

But you can't blame the dogs. It's not as if they choose their own names. Goodness knows what they would pick if they had the choice. There's that great Gary Larson cartoon where the first frame is titled 'The Names We Give Dogs', and a man is introducing his dog to a friend, saying, 'This is Rex, our new dog.' Then, underneath is a frame with the headline 'The Names They Give Themselves', and three dogs are greeting each other. 'Hello. I am known as Vexorg, Destroyer of Cats and Devourer of Chickens,' says the first. 'I am Zornorph, the One Who Comes By Night to the Neighbor's Yard,' replies another. 'And this is Princess Sheewana, Barker of Great Annoyance and daughter of Queen La, Stainer of Persian Rugs.'

Perhaps the most esoteric name among our morning circle of dogs is Gramsci, a foot-long conglomeration of white hair and willing teeth. He's named after the Italian Marxist philosopher and politician Antonio Gramsci, who was imprisoned by Mussolini for over a decade. Gramsci died in jail in 1937, but not before he'd written more than 3,000 pages of leftist political theory from behind bars.

I had no idea about any of this or who the original Gramsci was when his namesake first arrived at the park, and for several years I assumed the dog's name was just something a bit cute that its owners made up. Then I overheard a conversation between two other dog walkers with much greater general knowledge than me, and

GRAMSCI
THE MARXIST PHILOSOPHER

GRAMSCI
THE OTHER ONE

afterwards scuttled home to google him, feeling ever so ignorant. Mind you, I frequently feel a bit ignorant at the dog park, when discussion roams towards the rarefied as we stand and muse and posit and I hurl sticks for Cooper. Eva, who walks Gramsci for her daughter Esther, is a wonderful socialist, a charming bidder of the revolution. She made me feel slightly better about not knowing who Gramsci the Marxist was by saying that often, when she tells people what her dog's name is, they reply, 'Oh, I remember him.' At least I didn't pretend.

Meanwhile, Gramsci the dog remains less concerned with political philosophy than with warning off passers-by and worrisome new dogs at the edge of the circle.

SOME TAKE DOG NAMING TO extremes. There are all those silly pedigree dog names that make no sense and sound like an eight-year-old's attempt at romantic poetry. Here, for example, is a selection from a recent Crufts show: Braccorians Goddess of Love; Heaven's Mercy In Love with Dorea; Lochtaymore Bridget Jones of Tillycorthie; Dyrham Playboy of Chilworth; Whinchat Viking Flagship; Chartan Luna Love Good of Dubhagusdonn; Roughshoot Fire and Ice with Baratom; Hot Sensation's Orstone Cowboy; Bannonbrig Mr Brightside; Kiswahili Quantum of Solace; Pixie Attila Magic.

But some owners like to dub their dogs with a

multitude of names, despite them having not a drop of blue blood. When we first started going to the park, there was a woman called Jacky who had three dogs. There was a standard poodle called Lavender, a griffon named Otto of Okato, and a chihuahua named Lucy May Velvetina Morrinsville.

Jacky spoke French to her dogs. 'Lavender, ça suffit!' when the poodle wouldn't stop barking. 'Oh, ma petite,' when Lucy May Velvetina Morrinsville would shrink from the shadow of a monster dog. She also spoke Russian to them. That came from the time Jacky visited friends in the Soviet Union, fell in love with a Russian man and lived in Moscow for a year. But it was the era of Brezhnev and bread queues, and the chill of the Cold War became too much, so Jacky returned to New Zealand, where she studied Russian to keep the embers of her romance glowing. Fifty years and a million miles away, in the wide open spaces of Brooklyn, she practised the language of her faraway lover, her dogs multilinguists, her Moscow memories rekindled with every command.

But, more than anything, Jacky spoke the language of love. She spoke of panting passion between OOO and LMVM. She told of the night the two escaped to the wind turbine above Brooklyn, only to be found the next morning blissfully wandering the streets. They had eloped, Jacky said wistfully, the idyll of unleashed romance clear in her mind. My more sceptical mind, meanwhile, imagined the dogs passing the evening marking strangers' lawns and tearing rubbish bags asunder.

Jacky hoped for a litter of wee OOO–LMVMs one day. To that end, on 10 October 2010 (10/10/10), the two dogs were married in a brief ceremony. The bride and groom wore silk bandanas. Jacky said a few words. The newlyweds ate salami.

Otto of Okato would sometimes practise procreating on Cooper at the dog park. Unable to mount anything bigger than a loaf of bread, this amounted to clasping Cooper's back leg and going for broke. Cooper would look bemused, sensing that something undignified was occurring near his tail. Jacky would smile and sigh. 'Ah, mon petit.'

IF YOU HAVE TROUBLE WITH the difficult task of naming your dog, there are plenty of websites that aim to help you. But sometimes nothing quite works, nothing will satisfy your preconditions or overcome your prejudices. So it was with Moey, a Border collie crossed with a poodle. (Did Moey's owner, Anna, call her a Boodle?) When Anna first arrived at the park, we did the perfunctory greeting and I asked what her dog's name was. 'Moey,' Anna said. 'Like the champagne?' someone ventured. 'No,' replied Anna, almost apologetically, and then spelled it out. 'M-O-E-Y.' I gently enquired where that one came from, and

Anna explained it was a combination of the names of her husband's last two dogs: Mia and Zoe. He'd wanted to remember them, and combining their names for the new dog would help them live on and give him comfort. So, he and Anna had tested all the possible combinations and come up with this one, but added a Y to make it more like a proper name. There was a sort of awkward pause after Anna outlined this process. 'Whatever works . . .' Anna noted, seeking to fill the gap. Indeed.

Similarly Christine with her German shepherd pup Ashra. She and her partner had wanted a slightly German name, she explained, but everything they came up with sounded a bit harsh. They were, however, fans of the seventies German Krautrock cosmic space group Ash Ra Tempel—so that was the tangential trade-off that gave their pup its name.

And, hell, why not make up your own name? It's not as if there isn't a generation or two of children given names by their parents that are as bizarre as they are affronts to traditional spelling. Younique, J'Zayden, Jathon, Aphrica, Nevaeh (heaven backwards). Everyone wants their kids to be unique, and calling them something inexplicably weird sometimes seems the first step.

The beauty with dogs is that you can, quite literally, call them whatever you like. There's no higher power that can rule your name inadmissible or disrespectful on the grounds of religion, common decency or self-aggrandisement. There was that wonderful case of the girl called Talula Does The Hula From Hawaii. Man, I thought that was a fantastic name. But not so the New Zealand authorities, who eventually ruled it would be an impediment to the child's future. The Family Court judge was so disturbed by the parents' flourish when naming their daughter that he temporarily placed the nine-year-old under court guardianship so a suitable replacement name could be chosen. I wasn't so sure. I thought it was pretty evocative and unforgettable. I kind of look at my own mainstream name and think I'd like a little Hawaiian hula, a little South Pacific frill or flair somewhere in there.

ONE OCCASIONAL VISITOR TO THE dog park is a guy who often sports a wide-brimmed leather hat and calls his dog Son of Sam. This, of course, instantly conjures images of the weirdo who terrorised New Yorkers in the 1970s with a series of random shootings. When the culprit, David Berkowitz, was finally caught, he claimed he'd been forced to commit the murders by a demon who took the form of a dog called Harvey, who was owned by his neighbour Sam. Later, Berkowitz admitted this was all just some exculpatory nonsense he'd made up.

Anyway, the first time I met Son of Sam, a sort of curly, shaggy, spoodly labradoodly mix, I asked about his name.

'Oh no, his name's Max,' said the dog's owner. 'His father was Sam, though.'

Just as names don't always denote a dog's character—although sometimes they are alarmingly accurate—nor can they be trusted to indicate gender. One day at the park, up romped a sort of Milo-coloured kelpie. 'Bruce, come here,' shouted the dog's owner, dressed in camouflage fleece as if he'd just returned from a damp morning's duck shooting. Bruce circled the pack suspiciously, hackles up. 'He's a lovely-coloured dog,' said Barbro, breaking the ice with the newcomer.

'It's a she, actually,' the owner replied.

'A she called Bruce?' I asked, trying to appear nonchalant.

'Yeah, she used to be Elvis, but she didn't like that,' he said. 'So we called her Bruce.'

Matthew, who comes to the park with his bulldozer of a Lab, Louis, sometimes used to bring his mate's dog Bob. Bob was a collie with a coat that was like several colours of shagpile layered on top of each other, and moved slowly, reluctantly, as if going for a walk was requisite torture. Usually, there was a gap of 50 metres between Matthew and Louis and the panting collie. Bob was owned by a former New Zealand cricketer, and it was his second dog called Bob. Both dogs were girls. He also had a cat called Cooking Fat—'instead of him calling it Fucking Cat,' explained Matthew.

Gareth has Iggy. Iggy is a girl. Gareth is from south

Wales but is a shirt-wearing Tottenham Hotspurs supporter and they were initially going to call their dog Nayim, a former Spurs player whose name the kids used to chant. But on the way to pick her up, Iggy Pop was on the radio doing 'The Passenger', and the kids thought that fitted—Iggy Pup. So it was—but of course you might be forgiven for initially assuming she's a boy.

Just as you might assume that white and fluffy Snowflake was a girl. Nope. Snowflake is a boy.

But what about the traditional dog names, the ones that were almost synonymous with dogs decades ago? Lassie, Rover, Spot, Fido. Where have they disappeared to, other than when dogs are collectively joked about or disparaged? And what about Rex, a king of dog names once upon a time? Di from our dog park reckons her family had a string of them when she was growing up—every dog of theirs was called Rex. But I've never met one. Newly unfashionable, supplanted by pretentiousness, it's truly a shame.

Anyone who's read author and cartoonist James Thurber's 1935 *New Yorker* essay 'Snapshot of a Dog', about the bull terrier called Rex his family had when he was a teen, would equally lament the name's current obsolescence. Thurber's paean to Rex recalls him as 'big and muscular and beautifully made', an irredeemable cat killer but otherwise a fighter only when provoked. When goaded thus, Rex never lost, clamping his jaws on to his opponent's ear and holding on for hours. One memorable altercation was only resolved by the local fire brigade's intervention, hoses unleashing a torrent that even Rex stood little chance against. Thurber's Rex was also a tireless retriever, often of improbable neighbourhood objects. One time, it was a chest of drawers from somewhere down the street that Rex was grunting to manoeuvre onto the porch late one night when Thurber discovered him. Rex's end is harrowing—the essay is online, so search it out when you're in a resilient mood. In his final hour, Rex displayed the bravery and honour we'd like to associate with such a noble name.

As a tribute to all those noble Rexes, it'd be great to see a resurgence in the name. But while Bella, Charlie, Max and Ladybug reign, I fear it will be some time coming.

2.

The people we meet with them

I was like pretty much everyone who arrives at the dog park for the first time with their new pup—dog and owner equally timid. You're unsure whether to let your dog off the lead, because you think it will get beaten up by all the bigger dogs, or will run away, immune to your remonstrations and pleadings to come back. But you let them off, and within seconds they're surrounded by the other dogs, absorbed into that greeting ritual, that almost balletic circling of each other, slowly rotating, nose to tail, then moving on to the next dog. Within minutes, they're off scampering with the gang, making new mates and learning how the park hierarchy works.

And then it's your turn. Your turn to march towards strangers and hope for a friendly reception. Virtually without fail, you'll learn the name of someone's dog before you know theirs. It's almost as much a part of park protocol as the bum-sniffing, the human version of circling at a distance while you size up a newcomer. And, let's face it, it's the perfect icebreaker for strangers: You've got a dog. I've got a dog. What are their names?

So you find out, and enquire how old their dogs are, and what type they are. You discuss their habits and where they came from. And, once this introductory script has been completed, then the time seems right to ask the person who *they* are. I've puzzled over this process and its oddness, wondering why we aren't a bit more welcoming to the people themselves straight off. It's not that there's any etiquette. It's not that it's deliberately cool. It's just the way it seems to happen, time after time.

I can't remember exactly who was at the dog park the first time Cooper and I turned up, but Barbro would have been there. With her ruffian of a cairn terrier, Harry, she remains a fortunate constant at the park and in our lives, the nominal mayoress of the park, and someone it's a joy to see appear at the top of the steps coming from Aro Valley each morning.

Barbro grew up in Sweden, where her father was a famous respiratory doctor and her mother a GP who practised until she was 84. At high school, Barbro had science lessons in a class where the hyoid bone (attached to the tongue) of the last man executed in Sweden sat on a shelf. Johan Ander was convicted of murdering a woman during a robbery in 1910 and was guillotined, then his body dissected for science and various parts disseminated to schools throughout Sweden for anatomy lessons.

What effect this ghoulish pragmatism had is unclear, but Barbro chose not to follow her parents into medicine. Instead, without telling them, on a school trip to Switzerland, she sat the entrance exams for a prestigious translators' school, and spent four years studying in Geneva. She speaks five languages perfectly, but her life has been largely lived using the complex conjunctions of English, after meeting and marrying a New Zealand diplomat who'd been at Cambridge with her brother. How things swing on such chance.

Upon arriving in New Zealand in 1966, Barbro was taken to meet her husband's parents in Oamaru. From the Continental to the provincial, Europe's swinging sixties to stultifying North Otago, one can only wonder at the wrenching dislocation. Her in-laws were not without means, though, so every lunchtime the four of them would eat at the Brydone Hotel, entering its Victorian whitestone to be treated to the restaurant's pièce de résistance, steak à la Hawaii—two canned pineapple rings atop a burnt bit of meat.

Then, each night, Barbro would endure her mother-in-law's limited cooking skills: lettuce leaves with condensed milk dressing drizzled over them, tinned beetroot and either corned beef or tongue. Presumably there were some celebrated local potatoes somewhere in the limp, repetitive mix.

The couple's first posting was to Bonn for four years,

which was evidently wonderful. Then they came back to New Zealand, where things weren't so wonderful for one reason or another. During their next posting, to Tokyo, Barbro and her husband separated, and she eventually returned to New Zealand with their two children.

She'd met Ross Harris, a music lecturer at Victoria University, before leaving for Japan, and soon after Barbro arrived back in Wellington they got together. Everyone said it wouldn't work. Five kids between them. So very different. While Barbro had been to the football world cup final in Sweden in 1958, and seen and screamed at The Beatles in Stockholm in 1963, Ross had grown up in a Canterbury farming family, renounced sport in favour of intellectualism, joined his school's brass band at fifteen in order to get a uniform, played the tuba and considered The Beatles beneath him. When the group, by then stirring worldwide commotion and delirium, visited Christchurch in June 1964 Ross discounted them with something approaching disdain. Serenely biking through the city centre, he passed the crowds shouting and swooning outside the Clarendon Hotel on Worcester Street, desperate to glimpse The Beatles. He couldn't comprehend the fuss, and with his classically trained nose in the air, carried on to the library to return some Stravinsky scores. It wasn't until *Revolver* came out two years later with a classical horn player on it that Ross realised these guys might be worth a listen.

Barbro became a librarian at Victoria University, and Ross has become one of New Zealand's most renowned classical composers. The cynics be buggered—all that talk about divorcees and scarlet women and the scandal of it all—Barbro and Ross have been ever so happily together for more than 40 years now.

Barbro's first dog had also been a cairn terrier. Her family chose that breed because it featured on the front cover of *The Book of Terriers* that she'd had as a child. But at that time there were few cairn terriers in Sweden, so they found a breeder in Norway and the puppy arrived by train. Sadly, its association with wheeled transport didn't end there—it was later run over by a car and killed, scooped from the road and carried inside by her sister in a plastic bag.

Harry has less traffic to negotiate and reasonable road sense. Barbro says, 'He's very wilful. Well, actually, he's very disobedient.' But he has remained her company and comforter for over ten years, ever since Ross gave Harry to her for her birthday, Barbro indulging Harry's modest wants and burying her head into his fur when consoling is needed.

Barbro and Ross also have another dog, a tiny black Affenpinscher named Katie, who has a face like a capuchin monkey and is devoted to Ross. She only makes it to the park on special occasions, where her self-important yapping pierces the baritone barks of the rest of the pack.

When the grass is long, Katie almost disappears among it and you fear stepping back and treading on her, instantly rendering her a quadriplegic. She cost over a thousand dollars and, given she weighs just a few kilograms, pound for pound she's the most expensive dog at the park. When you stroke her it's like fondling gold.

Barbro and Ross have always had dogs. Before Harry and Katie, there was Mork, another Affenpinscher who might or might not have been the result of an incestuous accident. When Barbro and Ross went to get Mork, the breeder wasn't sure they were the right people to adopt him, despite their credentials and character. So the breeder went away to consult a medium—in the States—to see if they were suitable. And, sure enough, the American medium came back and said he'd spoken to Mork and he was happy to go with Ross and Barbro and be their dog. When we've reached the point where mediums oversee dog adoptions, we're fast approaching a land called lunacy. Sadly, Mork had severe breathing problems and lived for only seven years.

One senses there will be other dogs after Harry and Katie, though these are things we never discuss. But the urge is strong. One day, Barbro made her way up the path and spied a gorgeous, fluffy young Border collie named Max. 'I want a puppy,' she said with a surprisingly determined glimmer in her eye. 'I'm going to be like one of those mad women who snatch babies from hospitals.'

Barbro is, however, the kindest of people, though she can be curt when common sense demands it. When one of her stepsons started proclaiming the wonders of the 5:2 diet he was on, Barbro replied that she, too, had discovered a new diet. 'Ooh, what's that?' asked the stepson eagerly. 'The eat less diet,' remarked Barbro sharply.

Our conversations at the dog park are wide-ranging and worldly, covering the personal, political and practical. Every day provides an elucidation of current events and an education for me, because Barbro's interested in everything and knowledgeable about most. As we stand there, gazing over the harbour, one eye on our miscreants, one on the skyline, Barbro will talk of prison reform, football, her cynicism of political leaders. Soon after I met her, she announced how incensed she was about some TV billboards that screamed 'It's the story that counts' alongside a giant photo of a flak-jacketed broadcaster. 'It's not the story that counts,' Barbro railed. 'It's the *truth*!' That was the kind of proclamation a journalist loves to hear.

When her granddaughters Mia and Lotta would visit from Auckland for the holidays, she'd bring them up to the park each morning, if they could be prised from bed. And every day she'd pose them a philosophical challenge, like: Why do we pay tax? Should we eat meat? What is the role of nuclear weapons? It seemed such a wonderful alternative to holiday entertainment via an iPad.

Years ago, aged 55, Barbro got a tattoo, in an act of delayed rebellion. A small hippopotamus now sits on her left shoulder—the spot the tattooist insisted would be the least painful.

Beyond the skin, most people's dog park attire is necessarily utilitarian and unglamorous: gumboots, coats, past-their-best jeans. But Barbro always looks elegant in a Eurostyle way, despite having to wear Birkenstocks in all weathers, because her heels won't allow closed shoes. Sometimes a green Marimekko handbag from Finland is slung over her shoulder, which certainly raises the dog park's accoutrement stakes beyond the normal pocketful of poo bags and stash of treats.

Barbro has come to love New Zealand, but misses Sweden's winters. The cold is dry there, she says. When it snows, you can brush it off your coat. Everyone's house is warm. There's good and reliable public transport that takes you to interesting places instantly. Here, winter is chilling and damp and lingers. Barbro once lived in a flat off Tinakori Road that was so dank it had glow worms in the kitchen. Sometimes, when it blows hard at the dog park, Barbro will reach out to the nearest pōhutukawa branch to steady herself, and think fondly of the homeland she left more than 50 years ago and her family there, gathered at their summer house on an island in the Stockholm archipelago.

Barbro makes jewellery under the careful eye of Aro

Valley goldsmith Dorthe (who also comes to the park with her puppy). She studies Latin with a group who gather at each other's homes and translate Virgil. But much of her time is spent looking after others, caring for friends. Frequently, she'll arrive at the park of a morning and announce, 'I can't stay long today.' And I'll quiz her and demand she remain a bit longer, claiming it's for Harry's sake but knowing it's really for mine.

Then she'll be off, off to visit someone needing help, or to take a train somewhere to meet a friend.

One regular appointment she used to keep was to see an old work colleague, Lynette, who had no relatives here. In the sixties, Lynette and her mother had come from England to New Zealand for a new life. Lynette never married and became what some would consider the caricature of an eccentric spinster. At one time, she was found to have 30 cats—all in various stages of ferality and inbreeding. Eventually the council came and removed or destroyed them all. Barbro told her, 'You can't own 30 cats, Lynette.' To which Lynette replied, 'I don't own 30 cats. There are 30 cats that allow me to feed them.'

But then Lynette suffered a stroke and was left able to say only two words: bugger and lovely. Sometimes, she'd get them mixed up and, when you'd tell her somebody had died, she'd say, 'Lovely.' Her limited vocabulary inevitably drew attention. One day, Barbro took Lynette in her wheelchair to Wellington's upmarket department store Kirkcaldie & Stains. As they moved slowly along the aisles of expensive wares, Lynette was chorusing 'Bugger, bugger, bugger,' alarming all the KKK (Karori/Khandallah/Kelburn) matrons who were enjoying tea and tiny cakes.

Barbro would visit Lynette at her aged-care facility, Sprott House, where she'd sit with her, read to her, watch TV series with her. Lynette died in 2017, aged 82.

Sometimes, Barbro would take a bus to Hawke's Bay to visit another former workmate, who'd become New Zealand's oldest sex offender, well into his eighties, and was in solitary confinement serving a five-year sentence. It was an unlovely experience for Barbro, but he had nobody else.

Then there was Barbro's friend Pat, a great Labourite and friend of the Langes who, even in ailing health, was determined to see a change of government in 2017. So, as soon as early voting opened, Pat cast her vote in Ōhāriu, hoping to see Labour's Greg O'Connor replace United Future's Peter Dunne, and Labour triumph overall. But, just a week before election day, Pat died. Barbro had talked to her the previous day and offered to go over and help her, but Pat had said no, she was fine, not to bother. The next day she was found dead, sitting at her table.

Everyone initially assumed Pat's votes would still count, but it turned out that the votes of anyone who dies before election day become void. Upon learning this, another

of Pat's friends, Colleen, who was a dyed-in-the-blue-wool-of-National voter, abandoned all her personal and political ideals, went to her local election centre and cast her votes for Greg O'Connor and Labour so that Pat's wishes would be carried out.

When Barbro shared this story with us at the dog park, we stood around and mulled whether we would have done the same selfless thing out of loyalty to a friend. Most admitted they wouldn't—couldn't—have subverted their beliefs, not even once. I had to agree, and reluctantly accepted I was nowhere near as good a person as Colleen.

EVERY DAY, BEFORE 7 A.M., Barbro's brother would ring from Sweden. Growing up, he had apparently been a brilliant boy, academically stupendous but socially ill at ease. Then life's pressures had overwhelmed him, and he'd been in mental health facilities for the past 50 years or more. In all that time, his siblings had maintained contact and care. So, every morning, he'd call Barbro, let the phone ring once, then hang up so she would know it was him and she should ring back. When she did, he would grumble, reminisce, pity his situation. There was never a lot to say—the weather, the family, snippets of shared news. He'd want to talk of old times when they were kids.

This routine was repeated day after day, year after

year, and that morning call would be just the first to Barbro each day. Sometimes there would be three calls; sometimes six.

'Just once, just once it would be so nice for him to say something positive,' Barbro would say quietly. 'Like, "I had a good day today."' He never did. But she never stinted.

Once, he had tried to take his own life, by electrocuting himself, and after that had been kept under 24-hour watch. 'It's terribly sad,' Barbro would say, while noting it was also terribly unfair that some people with so much to give and so much to live for died early, while others who desperately wanted to die were kept alive.

I remember, one time, wanly replying that there was, indeed, no god. And Barbro looked calmly but intently at me and said, 'But there is dog. In Dog We Trust.' She was right. Perhaps if everyone had a dog, things might be a bit better.

In 2017, Barbro returned to Sweden to see her brother. Days after she arrived back in New Zealand, he died. And, of course, as difficult and frustrating as it often had been for her, she now found herself waiting at 7 a.m. for the phone call, which no longer came—and missing it. Kind friends offered to phone her at that time, to keep the routine, but of course it couldn't be the same. It was all about the gap.

IN 2013, WE DECIDED TO mark Barbro's seventieth birthday with a breakfast at the dog park—coffee and cakes and a dozen dogs flying around and 20 of us sheltering from the northerly. Balls and sticks and caffeine and merriment.

In the middle of all this, Barbro's phone went and she answered, and immediately switched to Swedish, all mouthy vowels and choked consonants. We assumed it was a family member from Stockholm sending birthday greetings. But no, it was her first boyfriend, reminding her that on that day in 1958, 30 April, they had been on a date—she was fifteen, he was nineteen. After four wives, he still held a flickering candle for her. How many people will get their very first boyfriend or girlfriend calling them from across the world when they turn 70? But then, Barbro is special.

ONE OF THE THINGS PEOPLE might not appreciate about dog parks is how much those who go there talk. About everything. Oh sure, a lot of it is superficial and fleeting, but when you see people up to five times a week, for many years, you get to know a fair bit about them. About them, their families, their routines, their habits and hobbies and history. In the time I've been coming to the park, I've discussed intimate medical matters, lived through children's depression and dramas, listened to the details of a relationship split just the night before, attempted comfort at the death of a partner, heard the harrowing and the heartbreaking.

There's a curious way the dog park disarms people. Inevitably, some very close friendships have developed, possibly because it's a space with no pretence. Dogs are great levellers: everyone picks up poo.

Kirsty and her mini schnauzer, Barney, arrived onto this canine common about six years ago. You can see her house on the far side of Aro Valley, and each morning she winds her way down the steepest street and up the steps to the park, where Barney sits patiently till told he can run wild. Around the time Kirsty began coming to the park, her husband, Ed, a recently retired lawyer, was diagnosed with Alzheimer's. Ed is great. He grew up in England, saw Hendrix and Cream in the sixties, lives for Leeds United F.C., and came to New Zealand in his forties. If you met Ed, you might not immediately realise he has Alzheimer's—but, of course, things are often different at home.

And there were other things, too, that Kirsty had to cope with and care for at home. Her younger son, Dan, battled with mental health issues, often struggling just to have a happy day. He'd had interventions and treatment and medication. But the Ritalin wore off quickly. One time, he took all his medication on one day. He had a really good day. To hide the fact, he substituted the missing medication with the cat's heart pills, which looked very similar. (I hasten to add that Arthur, the cat, had recently died, so no longer needed the pills.) Kirsty eventually discovered Dan's sleight of hand and he fessed up. But how to be angry at him, when all he wanted was to have just one good day?

In March 2016, Nikki and I were heading south on the ferry for Easter and had just entered Tory Channel when I got a call on a scratchy line. It was Barbro, and at first, I thought she said Kirsty had died by suicide. Then, she repeated herself and told me it was Dan.

That morning, Barbro had met Kirsty on their way to the dog park, and Kirsty had said, simply, 'We lost Dan yesterday.' At the park, everyone held hands and hugged— everyone else probably slightly amazed Kirsty could even face people. But then, the park has always been her solace in so many ways, a sliver of normality on the heavy days, a reliable circle of cheer and companionship.

Dan's funeral was after Easter, and I did a quick head count of fifteen dog park regulars who arrived at Old St Paul's church. The pews were narrow and hard, the coffin unvarnished pine with messages to Dan written on it in marker pen. Kirsty looked so tiny. There didn't seem enough of her to bear the weight of her family, not a lot of space for resilience to reside. But when she spoke, largely off the cuff, she was amazing—remembering her dear son, the cheeky livewire, and how his illness had grabbed him and dragged him down over the last seven years. And how the family had struggled, struggled to get the attention of medical authorities and specialists, especially in the last month, when they knew things were seriously wrong. 'You only see them once a week or every three weeks,' Kirsty said to the medical staff she knew were out there in the pews, 'and Dan was very good at putting on a show. But we see them 24 hours, seven days a week, and see a very different person.'

She realised the message might be difficult for some, but insisted it had to be heard and spread, and that more needed to be done, that families needed to be listened to, that more money needed to be spent on mental health.

Others spoke of Dan's wit and charm, and love of music and looking good, and his hair, and his blue eyes, and his Mick Jagger impersonations, and his romantic streak, and his dyslexia and hard work to get his degree, and his love of partying, and how cool he was. And they played The Beatles' 'Here Comes the Sun' and we sang along, and 'Don't Look Into the Sun' by the Libertines, and 'Dream a Little Dream of Me' by Ella Fitzgerald and Louis Armstrong as he, then we, left the church.

Fuck it, he was just 28.

IN THE FOLLOWING WEEKS WE organised a dog park roster to cook and deliver meals to Kirsty. As you do. Just one less thing for her to think about. One dose of guaranteed vitamins a day. Three months before Dan's death, Kirsty's sister had died of breast cancer, on Christmas Day. The rest of the family only knew about her illness in the days beforehand. Then her father got cancer. And when her other son, James, came back from the UK after Dan's death, things weren't always easy.

But every day Kirsty would arrive at the dog park with Barney, and be positive. I couldn't imagine dealing with even one of the things Kirsty had going on in her life, yet I was daily amazed by her strength and cheerfulness and openness. Only once did I sense her pragmatic and optimistic attitude might slip, as tears started to pool in her eyes.

When my editor at *North & South* asked me to write the editorial one month, I thought about Dan, and it occurred to me that the last three funerals I'd been to had all been suicides. I doubted I could offer much to a well-traversed subject of tragedy—nothing, really—but I spoke to Kirsty about whether it could be something that might help wear down our indifference and misunderstandings about mental health. And she responded with the same encouraging positivity she always exuded. 'It gives Dan a voice,' she said.

We still mark the anniversary of Dan's death, usually gathering at a café after our morning meeting at the dog park. And later, Kirsty and Ed and James and their daughter Kate will go to Lyall Bay, which Dan loved, and eat KFC—Dan's favourite meal.

YOU GET TO KNOW PEOPLE so well that virtually nothing is off limits. I remember the morning Barbro arrived at the park and announced, apropos of nothing, that Denmark was going to ban bestiality. That got the morning off to an unforeseen start. Who'd have known they even allowed it? Remarkably, they did and this had apparently led to a rise in Denmark's popularity in the underground animal sex tourism trade, partaken by zoophiles. Denmark's Minister of Food and Agriculture at the time, Dan Jørgensen, noted the harm being done to Denmark's reputation—and the animals.

But what was equally surprising was that a recent poll had revealed only 76 per cent of Danes supported outlawing bestiality. The other quarter seemed to be taking some convincing. Among them was the president of the government's Animal Ethics Council, Bengt Holst, who argued it wasn't their position to moralise. Scandinavian liberalism is renowned. Barbro once told me that in the seventies, when Sweden was leading the way in permissive change and sex clubs were becoming more open, she saw a sign at a peep show offering half-price for beneficiaries—so even poor pervs were catered for. But in the case of Denmark's bestiality laws, we all felt some severe moralising was just what was required.

Conversation then switched to other less-lovely European countries. Barbro nominated Belgium, which her first husband reckoned was so charmless that 'if it wasn't there, it'd be quicker to get to where I want to go'. Jeremy, who had the gorgeous black collie–Lab, Lola, seconded this and cited it as the least likely place for vacations. 'Nobody says, "I'm going to Belgium for three weeks", like they do, say, Thailand or Bali or the Gold Coast. What do you think of when I say Belgium? One word.'

'Chips,' I replied.

'Yes, and?'

'Beer,' I ventured.

'And?'

I was lost.

'Paedo sex gangs,' Jeremy replied helpfully. 'Nobody says, "I'm going to Belgium, because I want to see the house where Marc Dutroux kept those girls in a dungeon."'

I love Jeremy. Others sometimes find him a bit aloof, then sometimes a bit forceful in his opinions. I've always found him fascinating and fun. He admits to three passions: music, food and rugby. He works at Cuba Street's Slow Boat Records, has been in bands for years, does a Friday music slot on RNZ National with Kathryn Ryan, did a food blog on *Stuff* for several years, and knows a whole lot about rugby. A real lot. I just listen and soak it up and laugh.

One time, he turned up at the park eating pizza bread for breakfast. 'Le Moulin—isn't it the best bakery—anywhere?' he cried, then launched into an early-morning lecture on how we spent endless time ensuring diversity in what we ate for lunch and dinner, but almost always had the same thing when we got up. 'The tyranny of breakfast!' he trumpeted, as we walked back up the hill to our cars, calling our dogs. Lola was rolling in something on the far side of the park. 'It's probably just mud,' I offered weakly. 'It's never just mud,' Jeremy replied, as Lola raced back to his side, her coat flecked with something indeterminate, ready to accompany him to work, her face a mix of glee and guilt.

GEORGE WAS ANOTHER WITH STRONG opinions, and someone others didn't always know how to take. When we first got Cooper, George and his stroppy piebald fox terrier, Tonto, were regular fixtures at both the dog parks we'd go to. George was unmissable with his flowing white hair, white shirt with sleeves cinched by cufflinks, khaki camouflage pants held up with braces, wide-brimmed hat and rapid-fire, bellowed cynicism.

George scared some with his bellicose assessments of life, and turned off a few who took offence before taking the time to get to know him. But I thought he was wonderful. In return, he would not so much shower me with abuse for being a journalist as attempt to drown me with it, holding my head under as he ranted about my dishonourable trade and practice of it, eventually ending with a laugh that could be heard across the park and down into the city on calm days.

George had worked as a science technician at Victoria University, but when they made him redundant he set up an intriguing business making fish, bird and animal skeletons from his Brooklyn home. To do this, he would take carcasses, strip most of the meat from them, let the larvae of flesh-eating leather beetles clean off the rest, degrease and bleach the bones, then set about the intricate business of articulating them into their original form. He sold the completed skeletons around the world to museums, universities and vets. While George saw them as 'beautiful pieces of biological architectural art', many recoiled from them, 'because they associate bones with their own mortality', he told me.

'You can get a piece of wood and drive a couple of nails through it and somebody can call it art, but you can't show them bones and skeletons because that's not art—that's just plain bloody horrible.'

Looking somewhat like the crazy scientist, Doc, from *Back to the Future*, George was often misunderstood. One time, he went to collect a two-metre stingray from a fisherman in the small Wairarapa settlement of Ngawi. When he arrived, the village seemed deserted. George, who carries a notebook and pen because he's forgetful, eventually spied someone and approached them, only to be assailed with furious fuck-offs. 'Get away, you bastard! You bastard Mormons, you never leave us alone! You keep coming back here, you bastards . . .' Eventually the fishing boat skipper arrived home with the stingray and rescued George.

'Who's the stingray for?' I asked when he told me about it.

'Just me,' said George. 'No other bastard appreciates what I do, except me.'

Given his business was called Skulls Down Under, it was predictable that, when George rescued Tonto from Wellington's pound, he would describe him as 'a bag of bones'. And you have to wonder what Tonto thought the first time he was taken home, the air redolent with the decay and remains of other animals. But Tonto settled in quickly and soon ruled George's life and house, belying his name's translation of 'stupid'. Tonto would follow George everywhere, and bark incessantly if left home alone or in the car. After dinner, he would spend at least an hour on George's lap, then make it known he'd like to go to bed and would pester George until he was let into the bedroom. Of course, Tonto didn't sleep on the bed, but in it. If the electric blanket wasn't on, he'd bark and turn round in circles until George sorted it. If the blankets weren't turned down for him to get under them, he'd whine relentlessly. Once all this was resolved, he'd wriggle right underneath the covers. George would say, 'I'm going to write to *Scientific American* and ask how a dog can spend the whole night with his head down in the bed, when I can't spend five minutes down there.'

Tonto loved barking, and always had a lot to say for himself at the dog park. 'And always the same bloody thing,' George would chide. If people remarked on Tonto's yapping, George would tell them: 'You think this is noisy? You wait till he gets down the beach and see what a noisy bloody B he is then.'

'But you love him,' I'd say.

'Oh, and he loves me,' George would reply. 'I think there's a marriage proposal coming soon.'

I once greeted them at the dog park and bent down to give Tonto a tickle. 'Hello, Tonto. How are you, mate?' I asked.

'Oh, just as obnoxious as ever,' replied George.

'Ah yes, but you wouldn't be without him,' I suggested.

'No way,' admitted George. 'You're not a man without a dog.'

GEORGE WOULD ARRIVE AT THE park hollering jokes from a distance. 'It looks like a prayer meeting here, you all standing around. Who's going to lead the service?'

Barbro, who'd known him for years, since they both

worked at Victoria University, would call out, 'Nice to see you, George,' and George would flash back, 'I've told you, you can see me any time you like—$175 for an unframed photo, $250 for a framed one, hang it over your bed, sweet dreams.'

It wasn't only at the dog park that George sought to startle Barbro. At the pharmacy one day, as Barbro waited to collect a prescription, George burst out to everyone there, 'This lady's a well-known addict!' Barbro just smiled, her sobriety unimpeached, her affection for George undiminished.

But others were less charitable, and George managed to get himself into a proper stoush over an art piece he was planning. He wanted to create a skeletal version of the Four Horsemen of the Apocalypse: two horses coming out of the earth, only half exposed; another horse with rider in full flight on the ground; then the fourth horse, also with jockey, flying above them. It sounded dramatic and forbidding. It sounded terrible and offensive, said Carol.

George already had the bones of two horses which he'd somehow accumulated over the years, sitting in sacks at home. But to complete the work, he needed two more, and his plan was to find a couple of middle-aged horses, have them nobbled, then strip them back to bones. They needed to be at least fifteen hands high and no older than ten years, because after that osteoporosis started setting in. Thus, the horses couldn't be doddery old dobbins on their last legs hobbling into the knacker's yard. George had a bloke lined up in Eketahuna who'd agreed to do the job, with George there to preside over the death and dismemberment.

Carol, who had a lovely Australian shepherd called Bobby who was a Zen master of Frisbee catching, couldn't control the normal perfunctory politeness of the dog park and told George what he was doing was disgusting. How could he call himself an animal lover if he was going to do that to a beautiful creature, she demanded. George fired back that she ate meat, didn't she? Carol said, oh don't go down that ridiculous line of logic, George, would you ever use Tonto's bones like this?

Oh no, said George, he'd never do a cat or dog skeleton. Which Carol thought stank of hypocrisy and skewed morals. As far as she was concerned, George had crossed the line from eccentric to sick, and she stalked off, saying she wasn't going to listen to any more of this ghastly rubbish.

Which was lucky, because George hadn't even got to the bit about where the human skeletons were coming from. They would supposedly be sourced from India, which Geroge said would be ideal because, being smaller, they would emphasise the stature of the horses.

The next time I saw George striding across the park in Red Bands, the strap of his straw sunhat knotted under his chin, I broached the issue.

'I hear you've been upsetting people with your latest plan, George.'

'Have I? Oh, well, people get upset about a whole lot of things I do, so I'm not too worried.'

As Cooper and Tonto barked at each other, I asked where the idea for his proposed art piece had originated.

'It came to me from boiled cabbage,' said George in his inimitable way. And there ensued, predictably, a long tale that began with George growing up during the war.

'The British don't know how to cook. They just boil everything into an abomination.' And, according to George, cabbage was the poster child for such culinary sins, particularly at Sunday lunches. If you ate your cabbage, you got to go for a nice walk along the river in the afternoon, he said. If not, you got packed off to Bible classes. Every Sunday meal included this overcooked green slime, and one lunchtime when he was about five George had refused to eat it. So his grandmother came around behind him, grabbed his nose, opened his mouth and began spooning it in. It was vegetable waterboarding, and afterwards George was told he'd be going to Bible class. And what were they learning, or being told about there? The Book of Revelation and the end of the world and the Four Horsemen of the Apocalypse—the mounted precursors of Judgement Day.

'I must have been listening, because for 65 years I've been thinking about it,' said George.

Tonto suddenly went quiet, possibly dreaming of equine offcuts.

George had no idea where he'd stage the artwork. He hadn't got that far, but it was an issue of minor consequence. 'Problems are just solutions in disguise,' he told me. I thought that was just a bullshit truism, but didn't tell George that.

'I suppose I'll be getting more people wanting to berate me,' he sighed, and I agreed he probably would.

'Well, I don't care. If we worried about what other people thought, and did what other people said we should do, we might as well go and die in a wet creek. Some people might think I'm mad, and I might well be, but I'm going to do what I want and bugger the lot of them.'

It was typical defiance from someone with too few years left to waste them trying to appease the crowd, and too many ideas left to see to fruition. But George also had a strong streak of provocation and happily set out to shock people. Barbro reckoned the controversy about his plans would quite please him, and he'd likely stoke it.

However, those upset that George was a butcher of noble animals only saw the caricature they wanted. They probably didn't know how he'd spent years rehabilitating and planting the banks of the stream that flowed near his home. Or that when the swamp at Tawatawa Reserve dog park shrank in summer to a few square metres of warm muddy liquid, George would go there every day to scoop out hundreds of tadpoles with a net on a long stick, and transfer them to a bucket to save them from broiling to death in fetid gloop. Later, he'd liberate them in another wetland he knew of, or in the pond in his backyard. He knew the types of tadpole by their Latin names and could explain the whole life cycle of the frogs.

Equally, his loyalty to his dogs and his gentle indulgence of them was extraordinary.

George's bravado was brittle. There was much to admire beyond the exterior of supposed grumpiness and throwaway insults.

ONE DAY, GEORGE ARRIVED AT the park and mentioned he'd been unwell. Three months of being crook, he said— polymyalgia or something, where his whole body locked up. 'I don't eat any more, I just take bloody pills!' he cried.

'Old age, it's a prick,' I ventured.

'It's a privilege,' George shot back, quick as a flash.

OF COURSE, NOT EVERYONE I meet when out with Cooper has a dog. One day at Waikanae, returning from our normal circuit along the beach and back via the river, we noticed a single whitebaiter in the estuary. He noticed us too. Even from 50 metres away, I could tell he wanted to have a chat—he started moving towards us and kept altering his course and pace to ensure our paths intersected.

His name was Tainui, and he had come down the road from Ōtaki. He hadn't had much luck catching anything, but figured he might as well hang out here because it was better than being back home. And the fact all the other whitebaiters had left the river meant his odds of netting a rogue shoal were greatly increased, he reckoned.

Tainui from Ōtaki could talk, you didn't need to prompt him. You didn't really need to participate, actually; just stand there and hear him. He talked of whitebaiting, naturally, even though I neither caught nor ate them. I suggested it might be harder for him to catch a feed these days because of overfishing, not to mention the increasingly shitty state of many of our rivers.

Tainui from Ōtaki shook his head. 'Nah,' he said. 'You know what it is? It's these chemtrails from planes. They drop poison and that's what's killing all the fish.'

I looked up into the sky. Cooper did too. We didn't see anything.

'Nah,' continued Tainui from Ōtaki, following our gaze, 'it all happens way over the horizon. But it's real.'

I was stuck for something—anything—to say in response. Thankfully, I didn't need to, as Tainui from Ōtaki happily sailed on. 'The government, they know all about it. But they hide it and do nothing. They reckon I'm a conspiracy theorist, but no way, I know about these things. I've read about it.'

I didn't dare ask where. I didn't dare encourage him on to another topic. I mentioned I'd better get back for tea and he nodded, then sauntered back to his net and checked it: not a single fish—poisoned or otherwise.

INEVITABLY, THERE ARE SOME DOG owners who it's hard to like. While that just reflects wider society, you foolishly imagine everyone at the dog park will be a kindred spirit. But no.

When Cooper was a pup, there was a man who always stayed apart on the far side of the park, flinging balls to his springer spaniel, who robotically retrieved them. I'm not sure where the rumours first came from, but park gossip had it that he used an electric-shock collar on his dog. Witnesses claimed to have seen the dog leap at the pressing of a button concealed in a bumbag around the man's midriff if it didn't instantly return the ball. There were mutterings of torture.

I hadn't seen the device, but given the man's humourless demeanour it was an easy slur to accept. Since he'd never chosen to acknowledge let alone socialise with anyone else at the park, he became known simply as Mr Zip Zap, the man who mechanically lobbed balls for his mechanical dog and electrocuted it if it didn't obey.

Occasionally, the balls would come close to us. Usually, the spaniel would win the race to them. But one morning

Cooper got there first, and of course trotted back to me with his trophy and wouldn't give it up. Mr Zip Zap grumpily stalked over and, after I extracted the ball from Cooper's mouth and apologised, he grabbed it and walked off wordlessly, back to the far side of the park.

Not long after, it happened again. I was throwing tennis balls for Cooper while Mr Zip Zap, hugging the park's fringes, was tossing tennis balls for his spaniel. Cooper, in a frenzy of flying balls and early-morning exuberance, got the wrong ball, brought it back to me and pranced around with his prize. Eventually, I got him to drop it, and, not wanting to throw it back to Mr Zip Zap because Cooper would just chase it again, I thought I'd walk the ten paces to retrieve our ball and occupy Cooper with that, before returning the spaniel's ball. At about pace five, I heard a 'Hey!' from Mr Zip Zap. At pace seven, there was a more insistent 'Hey!' and I turned to see him striding towards me with purpose—the purpose obviously being to retrieve *his* tennis ball. As he advanced on me, he brandished his plastic ball-thrower in front of him like a fencing épée.

'Hey! HEY!' he repeated, as I reached my own soggy ball.

'It's okay, mate, I'm not stealing your tennis ball,' I explained. 'My dog just mistook your ball for his—it's an easy mistake to make.'

There was a sort of harrumph from Mr Zip Zap, but without any good-natured theatricality.

'I would have expected you to call your dog off,' he grumped. 'It's all about control—DISCIPLINE!'

I wasn't smart or composed enough to offer an immediate riposte, as he and spaniel and precious tennis ball returned irritably to their park edge.

Call my dog off? Cooper had grabbed a ball, not a toddler or a flightless bird.

The incident had a predictable sequel, which I was desperately upset to have missed. One muddy winter afternoon, an irregular and slightly unruly dog named Jimmy happened to jump up on Mr Zip Zap's daughter, who was aged about twelve. The next thing everyone heard/saw was a *thwack*, as Mr Zip Zap belted Jimmy with the ball-thrower. When Jimmy's owner, along with Barbro and Ross, accosted him, there ensued a yelling match the likes of which happily occurs infrequently at the dog park—perhaps only when midnight drunks disagree over possession of the final Woodstock bottle.

The daughter was mortified and tried telling her dad it didn't matter, she wasn't really dirty. But Mr Zip Zap shouted at Jimmy's owner that her dog was 'INDISCIPLINED', and said he wanted her name so he could report jumping Jimmy to the council. Barbro responded that they were going to report *him* to the council, and declared he needed to go to anger-management classes. Eventually, they all snatched up their dogs and stormed off huffily, back to their homes where different degrees of discipline prevailed.

I hardly ever saw Mr Zip Zap after that. Ross said he met him one afternoon, and they chatted about sunsets and how Mr Zip Zap photographed them and sent the pictures to his son. It seemed incongruous with our caricature of him as a villain. But even the easily outraged can take time to appreciate nature's spectacles, you have to imagine.

3.
The places we walk them

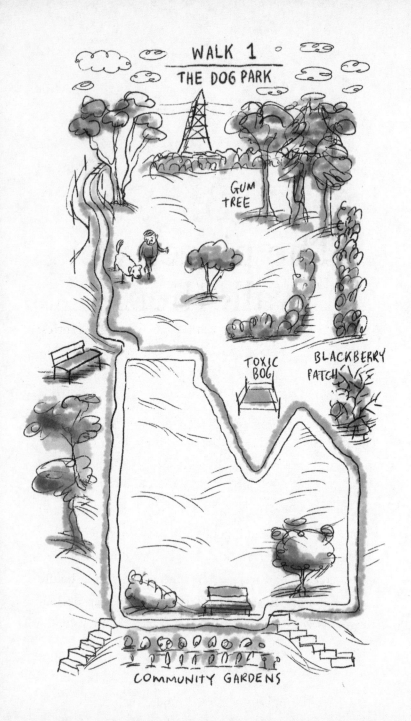

There's a simple, easy beauty in dog walking. Pretty much anywhere you can go, they can go. Exceptions occur when officious councillors and puffed-up bureaucrats ban them from city centres, and when native birds are nesting on beaches. But, in between town edge and tideline, pretty much anywhere is wandering territory. God, we're lucky, and so are our dogs.

The whole concept of urban dog parks, however, has become common in recent decades in response to the rise in dog ownership, and to provide interesting alternatives to pavements. But decisions about where these parks are situated are fraught. In a time when developers and politicians are screaming out for land to build homes on to counter the housing shortage, I often look over our dog parks and wonder, *How long?* How long before some witless, dogless dullard of a functionary decides townhouses would be perfect for Tawatawa Reserve or Tanera Park?

Tawatawa, where we often go in the afternoons, was actually a dump in the 1970s—Preston's Gully landfill they called it. When rain soaks the park's earth to capacity, occasionally you'll see an oily film floating on puddles and wonder what lies not far beneath your gumboots. On the park's sloping flanks, small rivulets that spring up in storms have eroded areas where dump detritus pokes through, like fossils uncovered by floods, or bleached skeletons exposed in the sand dunes. I've seen car springs, sheet-metal shards, jars and resilient plastic. But it's incidental and doesn't detract from the views or the enjoyment of walking there.

One wet afternoon, I met Dave, who was walking his boisterous black German shepherd called Molly. Seeing the iridescent slick on one puddle, which hinted at some buried car wreck or oil can leaching through to the surface, I stupidly muttered that the council only gave dog walkers shitty areas. 'I don't think it's shitty,' replied Dave. 'I think it's marvellous.' And he was so right. The park is an extraordinary asset that backs on to the town belt, meaning you can walk forever, or certainly for hours.

Tanera Park, where I walk Cooper each morning, has dormant demons too. It was the site of what they called the Ohiro Benevolent Home, built for the homeless and indigent in 1892, which eventually became the Central Park Hospital. It closed in 1975, the buildings were demolished, and the land returned to the town belt for recreation. But in the middle of the park is a small rectangle, maybe five square metres, which has been fenced off with waratahs and wire ever since I've been going there. I once met a guy who'd lived in the area for decades and he swore it was a pit where hospital staff dumped toxic materials. He also swore that he'd seen it frothing—the earth literally disgorging foam like some poisoned geothermal vent—when it rained heavily. I wish he hadn't told me that, and I now make sure Cooper never trespasses its scruffy barriers. But then again, if that's the price for the pleasure we gain from the park, it's small and acceptable.

Amenities are meagre at Tanera Park. There are two park benches, which largely service late-night drunks, if the frequency of abandoned RTD cans and bottles is anything to go by. On the bench at the bottom of the park, by the community garden, someone once scratched off the lichen growing on the wooden backrest and wrote a poem in felt pen.

And as I sat here,
blowing bubbles into
the night; the clock past
midnight and it was
Christmas day.
One whole year since she
kissed me goodbye
never to return again.

On one side of the poem was a tiny drawing of someone in a cap sitting on the bench holding what I initially thought was a glass of champagne, but think is bubble-blowing paraphernalia. On the other side was something that looked like a kitchen spatula or maybe a fly swat, but, again, I think was probably what you dip in the soapy liquid to create bubbles.

The poem remained there for a few months, but then one morning it was gone, scrubbed from the seat, its mournful verse completely obliterated. I couldn't believe it. Who could be so unfeeling, so insensitive that they'd dare touch another's emotions like that, when the writer had nailed their torn heart to a piece of public furniture? They'd used a semicolon, for goodness' sake. Of course, it could have been the writer who removed it, having second thoughts—or perhaps their true love had returned home. I really hoped so. But standing there in front of the wordless seat, I felt nothing but sad and angry at the park philistine who I imagined was responsible.

You can never stay sad or angry for long at the dog park, though. I need only walk to Tanera's upper level, and push aside the fennel and gorse that grows around the giant pōhutukawa to see the word 'JOY' graffitied in pink paint on its trunk. When I first noticed it, I debated whether it could be considered tagging or might be some Brooklyn gang slang. But no, I don't think so. Of course, it may be. It may simply be somebody's name, shouted along the pōhutukawa's brittle bark. But whatever it is, and as twee as it sounds, it happily reflects how I see the dog park.

CURIOUS THINGS OCCASIONALLY TURN UP at the park. There was an old metal chair that we used to tuck away under the pōhutukawa and bring out if Barbro ever felt frail. One day, a chipped and faded concrete pot-plant holder in the shape of a chicken appeared. Someone discovered a name tag for a dog called Maggie and strung it around the chicken's neck, and we stashed a supply of spare sticks for the dogs in it. But someone stole Maggie the stick chicken—or, at least, we presume that was her fate. Barbro's chair disappeared too. When I mentioned this to Jeremy, he made the point, which sounded almost like it could have come from 'Desiderata', that you only miss something if you've got something to lose in the first place. It was true, but the stick chicken and rusty chair were pretty much all we had at the park.

Of course, the park isn't just for dog walkers, though that seems its primary use. It's split from Wellington's Central Park by a sliver of road so runners, walkers, commuters and blackberry fossickers use it too. And the odd camper—perhaps homeless, perhaps in between accommodation, perhaps just enjoying the city's green spaces. Their small tents pop up, providing interesting smells for the dogs and, inevitably, the irresistible temptation to pee on the nylon corners. When the itinerants leave, there's just a flattened rectangle of yellowed grass and the prospect of discarded food scraps in the long grass for the dogs to investigate.

You wouldn't want to camp there for the peace, however. Nobody could sleep through Cooper and his mates—Hobbs and Hamish and Harry et al—barking their happy heads off as they negotiate the tents' guy ropes. I'm not sure if that's what caused one temporary camper, kitted in camouflage, to arm himself with a cricket bat, which he brandished one morning at a dog walker. Thank goodness it didn't happen to me—Cooper would have just thought the guy was preparing to throw him a really good stick and circled him, barking.

Mind you, I've been mistaken for a marauder with a weapon. One morning, I parked the car and let Cooper race down the hill while I grabbed a large stick from the boot to throw for him. As I hoisted the stick over my shoulder, a woman was walking up the path towards me and immediately said, 'You didn't even give me a chance to insult you, before you started coming at me with that thing.' I thought that was really quick so early in the morning.

You get to know the dogless regulars who stride down to their city jobs each morning, seeking sanctuary in their headphones, satchels and backpacks slung over shoulders, sensible shoes under chic office clothes. Some you get to know so well you wave to them, learn their names, each of you becoming a fleeting part of the other's routine. Others eye you with suspicion and maintain their distance—perhaps understandably, because to them you are just a strangely dressed man with a stick in one hand and a bag of excrement in the other, shouting 'No! No! No!' into the wind as you try to prevent your muddy dog leaping all over them.

There has been the rare commuter confrontation—a quick nip on an innocent passer-by's ankle, a bit of close-quarters barking, the odd regrettable muddy paw on freshly ironed clothes. It shouldn't happen, but it's almost inescapable. Some will say, 'Well, it's a dog park, what do you expect?' And there's a fraction of truth in that—well-heeled commuters and the dogs who struggle to heel can create an anxious mix. However, it's also a space for everyone, not just a domain for dogs. Though if you're wary of dogs, or wearing your best suit/dress/skinny jeans, perhaps take the path that skirts the dog park on your way down town.

Sometimes, the people you meet and the vignettes you come across are utterly random and wonderful. One morning, I made my way back to the car, towed in alternate directions by Cooper and his best mate, Hobbs, who I often walk. They wanted to sniff different things, and I was left grappling with leads and sticks and muddy balls and bags of poo. When I reached the carpark, there was a woman leaning back against her light blue Peugeot, playing a melancholy melody on her fiddle. She wore an embroidered black cowboy hat, a long purple coat and a green skirt that poked out beneath it and covered her ankles. Nobody else was around. I was an audience of one—not counting the dogs, who weren't as struck by the unreality of it all as I was. I was sure she must have seen me, but she didn't pause, the tune continuing under a clear sky and the hum of the high-voltage lines that lope across Brooklyn. The sounds of traffic from those late for work and hurrying down the hill provided a dull drone which seemed to accentuate her playing.

Eventually, she stopped and I clapped, and she turned and smiled. She was practising, she said. She was playing at the old bowling club nearby in half an hour, for a Feldenkrais session—a therapy that combines mental and physical exercise—and she was rehearsing while catching some sunshine.

'It's all about the joy,' she said.

I thanked her for the impromptu concert, wished her luck and loaded the dogs into the back of the car. As I reversed out and drove away, she was lifting her bow again—this time with only the tūī in attendance.

A DOG PARK IS AS accurate at telling the season as any calendar. Its changes mark off the months, its appearance a reliable measure of Wellington's undependable climate. Author Lloyd Jones once wrote: 'A Wellingtonian only really comes of age when he or she can look themselves in the face and admit, when it comes to weather, we live in an arsehole of a place.' I have that quote printed and pinned above my desk, just within my view out to Cook Strait and the foulness that frequently lurks over the horizon. Jones, it has to be noted, obviously tired of this arsehole city's weather and shifted to the Wairarapa. His quote remains true, though, and never more so than at the dog park in the dreary depths of winter.

But spring at the dog park is spectacular. The grass grows like bamboo and small dogs risk being lost in it, until the council mower man arrives and returns it to normal with slow, calculated circles of his tractor. There are snowdrops —or are they that onion weed?—and among them, along one bank, a single jonquil that's somehow sprouted and survived the year's dog action. I smile at it every morning and feel like guarding it, lest some thoughtless passer-by plucks it for themselves. There are buttercups and clover and the first honeysuckle flowers. The big gum tree sheds its outer skin, leaving lank strips of thin bark across the park, its trunk variegated in grey and brown and ochre.

Come summer, the dogs pause more often to cool off in the shade of the trees, where cicadas blare, though we're there too early for the worst of any heat. Blackberries ripen, golden-topped fennel crowds the pathways, sweet peas scatter themselves amid the undergrowth, and agapanthus bloom in blue and white. Harry revels in the freshly cut grass and squirms on his back, all uninhibited joy, all his bits and belly offered up to the sun gods. Barbro looks down at him, smiling beatifically, and says, 'To be honest, I feel like joining him, but of course you can't do that . . .' Sometimes, Cooper and Hobbs will lie down in the grass, panting and grinning and loving the smells the sun has unlocked. And it's so gorgeous that I'll sit down too and enjoy it, and let the boys flick their sticks and rugby balls at me until they tell me it's time to move on.

By autumn, the days are short and gumboots make their first appearances. Mushrooms sprout, dog shit turns to gloop in the rain and permanent puddles appear. For a while, there was a small lake at Tanera Park that turned muddy then fetid then vile, with tinges of teal and bubbles on the surface. The dogs weren't perturbed. They kept drinking from it and paddling in it, like game animals around a shrinking waterhole. So Ceri, another of the park regulars, and I collected fallen branches and covered it as best we could, hoping the dogs would avoid it, but within days the branches had disappeared. I thought some lazy bastard had nicked the sticks to throw for their dog. But no, someone had set fire to them. All that remained was black mud and a few charred sticks. Midnight hippies dancing around a bonfire? Vagrants needing April warmth? Bogan vandals? I looked for clues. All I found as I poked at the crime scene was the skin and stone of an avocado and a well-sharpened green HB pencil—not a

THE DOG DAYS

lot to go on, even if you were the Famous Five. I looked at Cooper. 'Lassie would solve this,' I told him. He sniffed at the burnt stumps of branches. He wasn't trying to get the culprit's scent, but to see if the remaining sticks were any good for me to throw. No, he decided, they were all too far gone, far too small. The only positive of the illicit inferno was that the evil bog had likely been sterilised.

And then winter. Days of filthy southerlies, hateful gales that test everyone's commitment. Barbro comes up the path, shouting into the wind, 'You'd think at my age I'd be allowed to stay in bed, warm and cosy, wouldn't you?'

'Yes of course,' I answer sympathetically. But of course she can't. A mixture of habit, conscience and a contract with Harry sees her out the gate and up the street in whatever horrors the weather gods choose to conjure. Usually, she can rely on company, but occasionally spirits flag and kindred souls are few.

One stormy morning, Diana found herself the only one at the park, slashed by wind and wet, her bedraggled dog, Bonnie, sheltering beside her. Diana later sent us all an email with a photo, blurred by raindrops, of trees being thrashed around, and the message: 'Don't we have "In All Weather" on the dog park crest? Was a lonely morning.'

A few times, it's just been me and Cooper. Me looking like a ninja dressed from an op-shop, in my black gumboots, black leggings, black coat and black beanie, and Cooper barking in the middle of the big green park,

his barks getting blown away, ending up in the trees—
along with half the sticks I've thrown for him.

Oh, the wind. Those shrieking nor'westers, which make
the power lines angry and see red tugs push grey boats to
safety in the harbour. We try to find shelter on the park's
top section, behind the tall and mature trees. Trees that
might fall and kill us, someone notes. No, I say confidently,
they've stood through many worse storms than this.

The others nod, but keep glancing towards the trees,
and I can sense their disquiet at our location.

'If we all get killed,' says Diana, 'they'd erect a memorial
seat for us, wouldn't they?'

The wind howls. We stand around uneasily. Sticks and
small branches blow down from the treetops, delighting
Cooper, who sees them as heaven-sent and urges me to
throw them for him.

TOWARDS THE BOTTOM OF THE park is a pile of wood-
chips, the type used for mulch, which is intermittently
replenished, presumably by council workers doing
pruning. After winter rains, the pile steams in the early
morning, little lazy plumes that disappear as the sun
dissolves them. To us, it's a mound of gardening material.
To Bonnie, it's a sauna.

Even Diana wouldn't claim Bonnie is genius material,
probably pulling up just shy of Mensa membership,

but she's the only one who's worked out the joys of the woodchip pile. As Bonnie trots up the park path, she'll sniff the mound's temperature, climb on top, then scratch at the surface till more steam appears. Then she'll lie on her back and roll—the joys of wet warmth radiating along her spine, one imagines. This process is repeated again and again: scratch scratch, roll roll, et cetera, et cetera. Eventually, she stands up, shakes, and catches up with Diana. She's sodden, covered in fragments of wood and redolent of pine. She stares at us, puzzled at why we're laughing, mystified as to why none of the other dogs have taken their morning ablutions at the park spa.

A SUNDAY AFTERNOON. A RAINY SUNDAY afternoon. Nikki is in Tahiti, a few thousand kilometres and about 20 degrees of temperature away. I'm understandably envious, as I don wet-weather gear and gumboots and head to Tawatawa dog park with Cooper. When we arrive, there is one other vehicle in the carpark. Cooper cares not a jot who is there or what the weather is, so long as the back door goes up, and I say 'okay' and grab the Frisbee and fling it for him.

We head up the hill on the bush track, slippery clay underfoot, fat drops falling from above. From up here, you can see the whole park with its looping tracks, new plantings and frog pond. And you can hear much of what's being said below, the park being something of an amphitheatre. A man's cry is lifting on the wind. I can't hear exactly what he's saying, but can tell it's a dog's name and that the man calling it is getting increasingly pissed off. I look down at Cooper, Frisbee hanging from his mouth, eyes fixed on me. 'Someone's going to get their arse kicked,' I say.

Cooper trots off and, as I hear the frustrated owner now bellowing from the carpark for his AWOL dog, I think how lucky I am to have an obedient dog who doesn't stray into the bush chasing rabbits or the enticing scent of decay, who comes when he's called. We loop the bush track, clamber over a recent slip and, by the time we get down on the flats again, there's only our car left and we've got the place to ourselves.

It's still raining. I look at Cooper and, confident nobody can hear me, ask, 'Do you ever wonder why there's nobody else at the park? Do you ever wonder why nobody else is bringing their dog out in the pissing rain?' Of course he doesn't. Like he could care anyway.

We do a final lap of the park, and just as we reach the carpark Cooper bounds away, waiting for me to throw the Frisbee one more time. I do so and turn towards the car. I look back. Cooper is on the far side of the field, standing over his Frisbee, making it reasonably clear he's not ready to go home yet and if I want the Frisbee I can come and get it. I think, *Fuck you, it's pissing down, you can bloody come when you're called.* I call him. He doesn't move. I tell him to 'bring it with you'—meaning the Frisbee. He remains still. I think *fuck you* again, and keep walking towards the car, sure that he'll come once he sees me disappear. I reach the car and he can still see me. I think, *Bugger, I'll have to hide so that he thinks I've gone and then he'll come.* I slip into the bushes, aware of how strange and suspicious I will appear to anyone who arrives. I wait, certain I'll soon see a flash of anxious black dog arrive, looking for me.

Nothing.

I whistle, trying to make it sound as if it's coming from far away so Cooper will panic and come.

Nope.

I call his name, hoping the wind will catch it and make it sound like I'm far, far away by now.

Nope.

I remember the man we'd watched earlier, yelling for his dog, and think how I must resemble him. I think how stupid I must look to anyone observing this sodden dog park theatre. I think how lucky I would be to have an obedient dog who doesn't stray and comes when he's called . . .

Eventually, I poke my head out of the bush, just as Cooper arrives. He trots over to the car, drops his Frisbee and hops in when I open the back door. He stares at me as if he doesn't know what I was shouting about. I give him a pat between his wet ears.

AFTER A YEAR OF WALKING Cooper at Tawatawa park I became moderately frustrated with the dog poo littering the place. Not too frustrated, as it was all biodegradable, I figured, and it was a big park. What irked me more was the dog walkers who would diligently pick up their dogs' offerings, knot the plastic bag, and then just drop it in the bushes. I always wondered what dog-shit fairies they thought would come in the night and spirit it away. Eventually, I emailed Wellington City Council, suggesting a rubbish bin should be installed at the park entrance, arguing the area was well used and it would be a simple way to keep it clean.

Imagine my excitement and delight when, a week later, I drove into the carpark and saw a freshly laid concrete plinth curing in the summer sun, then a few days later, a new rubbish bin sitting atop it. Well, not a brand-new bin. One that had been recycled from somewhere else, its wooden framing already faded, but I didn't care a bit. I gladly scooped up Cooper's first effort and overdramatically dropped it in the bin, taking a moment to glance inside and rejoice that there were two other bags already there. I felt vindicated! So vindicated that I enthusiastically picked up half a tennis ball that had been severed by the mower and added it to the bin as well. The people had spoken, I proudly told myself, and the authorities had been forced to act.

Three days later, I got a fuzzy phone call from someone

at the council whose name I asked twice and who I'm sure was called Forrest Graham although the voice definitely sounded like a woman's. She apologised for not replying earlier to my email requesting a bin, and asked whether I'd been to the park in the last few days and noticed what they'd done. I certainly had, I replied heartily, then began thanking her effusively for their speedy response.

'Well, I'd like to say it was because of your letter,' Forrest said, 'but we were going to do it anyway.'

I suddenly felt very deflated.

'As you know, we have a policy of not putting bins in dog parks,' Forrest continued, 'but in this case we thought it was being used by other people, and people were having picnics and that.'

I discerned this had been a slight moral and professional tussle for Forrest, and she was still reluctant to cede an inch to negligent dog owners who should, in her view it seemed, take their pets' crap home with them.

'You should see those bins on a hot day in summer, when they're full of dog poo,' Forrest went on. 'It's not nice. Oh, well, it'll be interesting to see how it goes.'

As if to reinforce her misgivings, she assured me people would still dump their poo bags in the long grass. I told her I didn't think so—if for no other reason than that I'd pick them up—and I suggested having a bin there couldn't do any harm, anyway.

But Forrest's cynicism and ideology extended further

into the council ranks, it appeared. The next day, when I pulled up at the park, there was a handwritten sign hung over the new bin. 'Take your shit home with you!' it demanded—possibly the work of a disgruntled rubbish collector, who now had an extra stop on their route. I ignored the sign's directive, and the next day it was gone. The rubbish bin, used by all, has remained.

EVERYONE INITIALLY FEELS A FRACTION self-conscious about picking up poo, but it just goes with the territory you walk in. You get used to the quick grab and inversion of the plastic bag, adept at nimbly knotting it then ignoring it. Some people use natty rolls of dull green plastic bags that are attached to their dog's lead. I recycle our newspaper bags, which are stronger but have the drawback of being transparent and thus incapable of disguising anything of Cooper's motion. But I'm not forced to hang on to it for long. There's a bin in the carpark at Tanera Park as well, predominantly full of the takeaway detritus of night-time yobs and the banged-up beer cans of small-hours carousers, to which I add my bag of dog poo.

And then someone takes it away.

We discovered this gradually, after reports of a stooped man in his seventies, in a white shirt and scuffed dress shoes, sifting through the bin's contents. He carried a black backpack into which he would load the multicoloured bags of dog poo, then shuffle down the path to the community garden.

I told Jeremy about this one day, as we walked back to our cars, and concluded by saying there could be only one legitimate reason for the man doing this. Before I could explain my conclusion, Jeremy proffered his own theory. 'To send it to politicians?' he suggested. I had to admit I hadn't considered this. But no, the man feeds his garden with what we've fed our dogs. I know this because he's told me, when I've found him rummaging in the bin and recycling our offerings. Others recoil at the thought of such composting, but I'm relaxed about it. I'm not eating the vegetables, and it's just manure by another name.

So now, when I meet the man, I simply hand him my bag of freshly collected dog poo. I did this recently, exchanging pleasantries and poo, him thanking me in his modest English and explaining once again that it is for his garden. Matthew stood at the top of the path watching. As I reached him, he was smiling and shaking his head. 'You wouldn't believe it. You wouldn't bloody believe it. You can give someone two bags of dog shit and they tell you "thank you very much".'

MANY FRIENDSHIPS THAT HAVE BEGUN at the dog park have extended well beyond that morning walk. It's the luckiest of things. Rituals evolve. We have pot-luck breakfasts of coffee and cakes at the park to mark people's birthdays. It's just a nice way for everyone to begin the day, especially the person whose birthday it is. Diana emailed us after we surprised her with breakfast one year, saying, 'Best dog park in the world.' I thought she might quite well be right.

And each December we have what's become known as the Dogs' Breakfast. It began the year I started going to Tanera, a few of us deciding it would be nice to celebrate Christmas communally at the dog park. And we've done it every year since, the number of attendees rising, the quality of the food now elevated to exceptional. Marita prances down in her Santa suit, as does Katie, Ross and Barbro's wee Affenpinscher. Other dogs trail tinsel, and there's the requisite group photo wherein the dogs are usually running amok. Everyone drinks a lot of coffee and swaps holiday plans.

At other times, we swap garden plants. We swap books. We swap the stories of our days—remarkable and unremarkable. The comfort that develops between us means the most private things become conversation. We know much about each other's lives.

To the outsider, we probably seem a peculiarity, a raggedy club, a gathering of the mildly obsessed. There's some truth to all of these assumptions. But, good grief, there's no exclusivity—no airs and precious little grace, apart from the dogs in full flight. However, we have been accused of such. Diana once reported meeting a woman who said she went to Tanera Park. 'Oh, so do I,' said Diana. 'What time do you usually go?' The woman replied that she went mainly in the afternoons. 'I used to go sometimes in the morning, but there's this group of people and they're quite cliquey.'

Oh, god. Cliquey? Snobs? That cut deeply. We'd always imagined ourselves to be equitable and open, welcoming of newcomers, having no proprietorial claims on the park or the conviviality that occurs there. But I can, unfortunately, see how that perception might arise. We are often found deep in conversation, and our loose huddle could seem intimidating. But I'd hate to think people wouldn't feel comfortable introducing themselves or letting their dogs get to know the regular gang.

Some people choose to avoid us, sidling around the park edge, their dogs reined in, as much distance as possible kept from us. At Tawatawa one time, a group of friends were standing around, their dogs careering and chasing and wrestling, and a bloke with a Rottweiler loomed into view. The others kept an eye on their dogs, lest there was any trouble. As the guy passed by, they offered the usual pleasantries, then the guy looked back over his shoulder and hollered, 'Bunch of handbags!'

Sometimes, my best efforts at being welcoming have been dreadful failures. One morning, a woman and her young son arrived with their six-month-old black Lab, who was all wet nose and quivering flanks and puppy fat. The pup was on a lead with one of those Halti head collars around her muzzle, which are meant to magically stop dogs from pulling on the lead. I naively asked the woman if her dog wanted to run around with the others, but she said no, her vet had told them that, until the pup was fully grown, she shouldn't be let off the lead because she'd jump and run and damage her joints. That was at least six months away, as it's sort of understood that puppies are fully grown at a year. I'd met others walking their tethered dogs in wide-open spaces who'd been told the same thing by their vets. It appeared well-meaning advice, and it was doubtless backed by some study or science, but it seemed completely impractical to me. So I gently commented to the woman that the views of her vet seemed to be in vogue at present, though it was hard to imagine pups would have been leashed till they were a year old when they were living naturally in the wild.

'But they don't have dog parks in the wild,' the woman snapped back.

The whole world is a dog park in the wild, I thought, but didn't dare say.

'And she's off the lead at home,' the woman continued. 'It's just here, where there are other dogs.'

Yes, here where there were other dogs racing around with huge smiles on their un-Haltied faces. Other dogs who were running up to sniff the pup and wanting her to play. Other dogs who were having a brilliant time. Meanwhile, the pup was lurching on the end of her lead, desperate to join them and rubbing her face along the freshly cut grass in an attempt to free herself from the Halti.

By all means, take your vet's advice. But it seemed almost cruel to then take your puppy to a dog park and not let it off with all the others. And I couldn't help wondering what happened after a year, when those perfectly formed joints were finally let loose after that crucial socialisation period when a dog learns how to behave in a pack had ended. What kind of socially stunted dog might you be left with? Of course, I raised none of these things with the woman, not wanting to disturb the park equilibrium on a bright morning. And she and her miserably shackled Lab never returned.

But far more often the initial greeting of a stranger walking down to the park with their new dog has resulted in happy friendship. I remember arriving for the first time at Tanera, knowing nobody, making diffident conversation. One of my first mornings there, Cooper, in a frenzy of pirouetting excitement at meeting Hobbs, took the legs from under Hobbs' owner, Briar, and sat her on the ground with a hell of a thump. So my introduction to Briar was an ashamed apology, which she took wonderfully calmly as she stood up and brushed the grass from her jeans. Since then, we've all become the best of friends.

What's that John Steinbeck quote? 'A dog . . . is a bond between strangers.' He wrote that in a book about travelling around America with his dog, Charley. In later years, it's been suspected Steinbeck invented lots of what's in the book. Even his son reckoned it was more fiction than fact. But there's absolutely no doubt about the truth of his quote, and Tanera Park's deep friendships attest to that and to how those bonds can evolve.

Mind you, ten years ago, when I first started going to the park, there seemed fewer people there of a morning—often just Barbro, Mary Ellen and her sedate cairn terrier, Mackenzie, and me, and sometimes Barbara with Hamish. There wasn't really a group, as such. Or that's how I remember it. Now we can often have ten dogs, sometimes fifteen when the weather is particularly kind. It can get chaotic, with dogs barking and owners barking orders and admonishments, and balls flying, and Barney making a break for the community garden's compost heap, Kirsty hurtling in pursuit. And, thus, you never manage to have an uninterrupted conversation, or catch up with everyone, or achieve wise consensus on the issue of the day after carefully dissecting it as a group.

Added to the mix, sometimes we have dogs turning up without owners. There was one owned by a builder who was working on a house in Brooklyn. The dog used to just take himself off, walk half a dozen blocks, then hang around at the park much of the day. Smart dog.

We've even had people turn up who don't have a dog, including a woman in a blazing pink top who said she just liked dogs and proceeded to try to grab anything that ran near her and fondle it. I admit, I'm sort of guilty of this behaviour too. I'm the sad-arse who goes on holiday and misses his dog so much that I veer across pavements and cross streets to say hello to random dogs, just to feel their fur slip through my fingers. But, weird and almost creepy as that might seem, I've never turned up at a strange dog park for a fix.

Some days, the park is so popular and populated that Ceri and I have joked about having to start up a separate group elsewhere in the park. I mentioned this to Jeremy one day, and suggested we'd have to start staggering people's arrival times to maintain a modicum of dog park decorum. Jeremy paused for a second and scrutinised the horizon. 'I think the park's big enough for all of us,' he said wryly and wisely.

EVEN BIGGER AND BETTER THAN the dog park is the beach. A beach is simply a dog park without boundaries. Its limits are set only by how far the sand stretches or how far beyond the shallows your dog's bravery takes it. Cooper lives across the road from a beach, but it's a disappointment to him, particularly because the council insists all dogs remain on a leash, which makes a legal walk there a small cruelty for dogs: several hundred metres of sand and sloping shingle, only to be kept from it by a metre of taut lead.

But further afield the beaches are wider, the sand softer, the councils more relaxed. On the Kapiti Coast, at places like Paekakariki, Raumati and Waikanae, Cooper's walks take him close to a heaven of sorts. He senses the beach's smells and sounds from blocks away—the surf, the salt, the prospect of a thousand driftwood sticks, that ossuary of trees along the high-tide line—his nose straining closer to the crack in the car window, excitement escalating. When we let him off his lead, he sprints down to the water's edge, turns, crouches flat on the sand and waits for us to arrive with a stick. If the stick isn't big enough, he will ignore the first throw, barely flinching as he stares back towards the dunes, back to where you've come from, to where you must return and do better when selecting the next stick. Once he's satisfied with your choice, he leaps the small waves to retrieve the stick, bounds back onto the beach with fur now slicked by the sea, and drops it about ten metres from us. Never *by* us, even though that would be simpler for everyone. But when you're filled with élan from being in the vast open space of a beach, logic is an afterthought.

Cooper then circles us as we fetch the stick and continue our walk along the beach. The circles are contiguous and regular in diameter. If you turn and look back where we've come, the pattern of pawmarks he leaves in the glistening sand is like a stretched-out phone cord. We fling the stick until we think Cooper has probably swallowed enough sea water, and then tell him that's enough. He feigns disbelief, but eventually drops it and trudges after us as we carry on up the beach. On the way back, he scoots ahead and finds the discarded stick, and the whole process begins again, in reverse.

But sticks and dogs and beaches are occasionally a dangerous mix, and when this occurs, getting close to heaven can take on a different meaning. One day, when walking Cooper and Hobbs along Raumati's beach, I found a magnificent stick, heavy at one end which made it easier to heave beyond the shallows. As we walked and played fetch, we passed a black spaniel who was sodden from swimming and showed a keenness to join our game. Lily was no match for Cooper's speed, but that didn't deter her from dancing around us.

On one backswing, as I went to hurl the stick seaward, I felt a small jolt. I looked around and there lay Lily, motionless on the sand. Dead. In the time it took Lily's owners to double back up the beach, it all became clear—I'd clunked Lily in the head as I wound up to throw the stick, and had killed her. Her owners approached, as I crouched beside her body. 'What happened?' they chorused, standing over me with looks that quickly swung from bewilderment to accusation. I knew what had happened. But it had been an accident and not my fault, I rapidly reasoned to myself. It was Lily who'd run up behind me, I couldn't see her, and she'd just got too close to the action. But, if I began to explain this, I knew any context would be lost and 'What happened?' would be quickly and simply answered: I had killed their dog. So I hesitated.

And, in that instant of weighing my options between honestly telling them about the tragic calamity and lying and pretending I had no idea, Lily twitched.

I held my breath, hoping it was a sign of resurrection and not a death spasm. She twitched again, then raised her head slightly from the sand. And then she was up, and wobbling off. She'd just been knocked out cold. Any further conversation between her owners and me was lost in an enormous wave of relief, and then curious thoughts about whether dogs get concussion.

Cooper impatiently dropped the stick back at my feet. 'Throw it again,' his eyes and tail said.

EVEN BIGGER THAN THE BEACH, and arguably better in Cooper's list of favourite places, is the bush. While you can't take dogs into New Zealand's national parks, we're lucky to be allowed them in other parks. One is Tararua Forest Park, more than a thousand square kilometres of bush and barren tops straddling the spine between Kāpiti and Wairarapa. We often go tramping there, and usually end up at a blissful campsite beside a river, where Cooper swims for sticks till he shivers and chases Frisbees till we tell him to have a rest. It is, for him, the ultimate dog park, and I've no doubt he wishes we could live there forever. Or most of the year, at least.

One Queen's Birthday weekend when the forecast looked good, we decided to head into the Tararuas for the weekend. When we reached our campsite, the whole valley was wreathed in river mist and there was still frost on most of the clearing, despite it being mid-afternoon. But Nikki built a fire, the not-quite-dry sticks hissing and popping, and Cooper snuggled in close to us and it. After dinner, we toasted marshmallows and I tried to be clever and stuck four of them on one multi-pronged stick. I was doing okay, and they were just about ready, when Cooper got interested. Not in the marshmallows, but the stick. Any other dog would have eyed the marshmallows, but not Cooper. For him, the pissy bit of mānuka barely bigger than a twig was the prize, so he nosed in and gently grabbed it. With four golden marshmallows at stake, I wouldn't let go, and a delicate tug-of-war ensued, as Cooper backed away with the stick and I hung on. Eventually, the stick snapped, the marshmallows fell into the mud and Cooper stepped on one of them. It stuck to his foot as he pranced off with the stick, and I threw the rest into the fire to burn brightly with sugary toxicity.

We tucked him up like normal under the tent's fly, but it was bloody cold despite several layers under and over him. Around midnight, there was a fair bit of groaning coming from him, so we unzipped the tent to see what the problem was, and in he flew. He immediately took up the prime position between us, grumbling if we cramped his space, stabbing our backs and stomachs with his paws as he stretched out. Eventually, we got some sleep—Cooper far more than us.

Just past dawn, he stood up, shook himself and made it obvious he wanted to go out. I opened the tent, thinking he needed to pee and out he toddled. After ten minutes he hadn't come back, so I looked out to see where he'd got to. There he was, a few metres away, sitting on the frozen ground, surrounded by frosty grass, his Frisbee in front of him. Another awesome day was about to begin.

THERE ARE ANY NUMBER OF arguments you can make for not owning a dog—lifestyle ones, economic ones, cat ones, hygiene ones even. But I reckon I could come up with a longer list of possible reasons why you should. Or might at least think about it. I mean, for many people, it's just not practical and others simply can't guarantee their lives will be stable or secure for the twelve or more years a dog will likely live. But, other times, having a dog wreaks near-miraculous changes.

My friend Becs lives in Dunedin and has a daughter called Rosa. Rosa wanted to be a vet but was petrified of animals. She had about twenty soft-toy ones surrounding her in bed, but would be paralysed by them in real life.

This, of course, presented a multitude of challenges if Rosa wanted to follow her career choice.

One day on the beach, Becs and Rosa met a man who was walking an eleven-year-old wire-haired fox terrier. The man said the terrier was the best dog ever and, a little surprisingly, the best pig dog ever. 'Never gives up,' the man said without going into details, which would have horrified Rosa. So Rosa patted the best dog ever, and that went very well. And later she announced she wanted one of those dogs: an eleven-year-old wire-haired fox terrier. So that's what they got, just a much younger version. But, even when it arrived, as innocent and cute a ball of coarse fluff as it was, Rosa was scared witless of it. It took more than a month for her to get used to the puppy, to feel confident around it, to fall in love with it. Now, of course, she dotes on it.

So does Becs. For years, she'd had back problems and tried a catalogue of practitioners and promise-making experts. Nothing worked. Their neighbour at Karitane, where they have a bach, happens to be a top back specialist and eventually Becs asked him for help. He told her, 'You don't need help. Just exercise and sleep.' One leads to the other, in some ways. So Becs began walking their new dog for 40 minutes every morning along the beach, once the kids were at school. After two months, her back had come completely right. No drugs, no surgery, no manipulation, no wishful massage. Just a dog, a beach and going for a walk.

4.
The dogs we meet with them

Miffy was a giant snowball, a blindingly white Samoyed, who appeared to be just a nose and eyes peering out of an exploding pillow.

Miffy was owned by Moggie.

Moggie would turn up at the park, dog lead looped around her neck, jeans patched at the knee, hands shoved into an old red-and-blue parka, a *Harry Potter and the Deathly Hallows* tote bag slung over her shoulder, looking like a cross between a tramp and a garden gnome. When the weather turned wintry, she would appear in a full-length Driza-Bone coat beneath which jutted gumboots, her hands warmed in welders' gloves, her face surrounded by a splendid scarlet woollen hat with ear flaps, which were knotted under her chin. Moggie taught children piano and guitar, and did country dancing. She fed the expanding flock of kākā that now resided in Brooklyn, and recorded whether they picked up treats with their right or left foot in an effort to advance avian science.

And she knitted jerseys—out of Miffy's fur.

Every month, she'd comb Miffy and harvest a supermarket bag full of hair—mainly the soft fluff from Miffy's belly and undercoat, rather than the coarser hairs along her back. This was then sent away to be carded—teased and combed and then blended with sheep's wool: two-thirds sheep, one-third Miffy. Then it was returned to Moggie to spin and knit, and sometimes dye with plants and leaves from her garden. Moggie claimed it was like alpaca or mohair, but silkier and stronger. Each year, Moggie retrieved about one and a half kilograms of hair from Miffy, the whole process having the benefit of cooling Miffy, particularly in summer when sheltering in the shade was her only defence. Moggie insisted dog-hair jerseys were a textile revelation. She had even made one for a friend, using their Border collie's coat.

At the dog park, the topic of just how comfortable each of us would be wearing a jersey made from our dog's hair was something that caused considerable discussion, with people's views displaying a surprising degree of squeamishness. Because, I mean, is there really any difference between dog hair and sheep wool or rabbit pelt or possum fur? Well, yes, seemed to be the answer from the dog park. Sheep weren't usually pets. Rabbits and possums were pests here. Everyone could see the fundamental logic of using dog hair, and the essential practicality of it, but few could get much further than that. Perhaps it was simply that we have a thing about jersey orthodoxy and their knitted limits: Just look at how David Bain is forever typecast by those vivid and vile things he wore—designed by him and knitted by his mother.

For most people, there was just some intangible emotional quotient that made the concept of a dog-hair jersey a step and stitch too far. Even the most open-minded among us weren't asking for Moggie's phone number to place an order.

Moggie always seemed so meek and cheery, so it was a bit surprising when, just before one election, she fired up as we were discussing the likely outcome.

'It won't matter, whatever happens,' blurted Moggie. 'We're all still slaves to the capitalist system. Nothing will change while we've got the wage system.'

The rest of us fell silent, and it became clear this was just an overture for Moggie's broader political treatise, which concentrated on the beauties of socialism and the evils of free enterprise. If you closed your eyes, it was almost like that peasant scene from *Monty Python and the Holy Grail*, with its talk of anarcho-syndicalist communes, self-perpetuating autocracies and exploitation of the workers. Then Moggie spotted I was wearing a T-shirt with Che Guevara screen-printed on it and seized on me as a comrade.

'I've got a poster of that. Had it on my wall in the sixties. Still got it. Would you like a copy?'

Somehow, from Cuban political ideology we got on to another of Moggie's pastimes: Scottish country dancing, with nary a slip between the Sierra Maestra and St Michael's church hall in Kelburn, where the local enthusiasts were holding a meeting that night. It was a come-and-try evening, Moggie said, noting you needed neither experience nor rhythm. A no-obligation opportunity to get down Gaelic-style, where you'd earn hearty applause just for being an honest trier, she promised.

With only about 30 in the club, Moggie was on a membership drive, and she pursued me up the path with the determination of someone selling window insulation or one of those charity muggers who leap at you on busy city streets. I couldn't think of many worse ways to spend an otherwise perfectly fine Wednesday evening. Exhibiting incoordination amid strangers? Pure hell. But Moggie wouldn't be deterred. By the time I'd loaded Cooper into the car and swung myself into the driver's seat, she was still saying she hoped she'd see me at the hall that evening for a bit of shindiggery. For everyone's sake, I stayed far away.

For a year or so, I didn't see Moggie and Miffy. Then, one spring morning, a mini Miffy arrived down the park path, Moggie being towed along behind with both hands on the lead. This, we soon discovered, was Zhanna. Miffy had died earlier that year. Always a scavenger, Miffy had a history of ingesting then disgorging inedible objects, such as tennis-ball segments. When a plastic building block got stuck in her stomach, it required an operation to remove it. And, when the same symptoms of some internal blockage came again, Miffy went in for another operation. This time, the vet only retrieved a collection of sticks and garden litter that had been hoovered up as Miffy snuffled through the undergrowth. But Miffy didn't recover after that operation, remaining listless and in pain. Three days later, Moggie decided to do the kindest thing and put her to sleep. She'd had Miffy for twelve years.

At just over 70, Moggie figured she was too old to get another pet. 'But I just missed having a dog *so* much,' she said, and before long she was contacting breeders and got Zhanna. Moggie gave her a Russian girl's name she found online, because Samoyeds were originally Siberian dogs used by nomadic reindeer herders. Zhanna was six months old and already a handful. Bred to pull sleighs, in New Zealand she was limited to pulling Moggie's arms from their shoulder sockets.

I greeted Moggie and suggested she let Zhanna off to run with the pack, but Moggie told me the last time she'd done that Zhanna had disappeared down into Aro Valley. Instead, Moggie mentioned she had a long training rope—about ten metres of twine—which she threaded through Zhanna's collar.

Now, it just so happened that on this particular morning we were celebrating someone's birthday, as we often do, with cakes and coffee—not so much a breakfast of champions as one of early-morning indulgence. To accommodate the assortment of treats, Ceri had brought a folding table, which was just above the height of most dogs' noses. It was both laden and flimsy. I could see the disaster that was coming.

As Moggie unspooled the training rope, Zhanna bolted. She wheeled left around those gathered by the table, the rope pulling taut behind their knees and threatening to topple the table loaded with date scones and cinnamon buns and muffins onto the ground. Some people grabbed their legs, others grabbed the table. Mayhem was averted just in time, as Moggie caught up, straightened the rope, unclipped Zhanna and let her free. Zhanna reeled and romped and never showed any sign of absconding—there was far too much action and distraction to be enjoyed with the other dogs.

In time, there would be Zhanna garments, but Moggie still had a stash of Miffy fur to knit into jerseys first. She even had some from her previous Samoyed, Snowball, who she'd had for fourteen years. Despite the slight strangeness of it, I could appreciate how making jerseys from her dogs' fur was a way of keeping the memory of each one alive, of keeping them close in the most practical fashion. It just wasn't quite the way I imagined ever wanting to do it.

WE HAVE ROYALTY AT TANERA PARK, or as close as a strip of scruffy Wellington town belt is likely to get.

Frida bounded down to the park one morning and into our small group of regulars. A Bernese mountain dog, her mix of black and brown and white hair flowed behind her as she ran, a giddy smile on her face. Her owner, Lara, was equally cheery and great company, and in the school holidays would be accompanied by her younger daughter, Scarlett. We watched as Frida grew, grew up and learned how to be a dog, how to interact, how to squirrel into the bushes on sniffing missions, how to play with dogs a tenth of her size and not overwhelm them. She was gorgeous and knew it.

In the paper one morning, I noticed the national dog show had been held over the weekend at Porirua and the supreme champion—Best in Show—had been a Bernese mountain dog. A Bernese mountain dog named Idaho, who, according to his owner, had 'incredible bones, a stunning head and his movement around the ring is just unbelievable'.

I told all this to Lara, who I thought would be chuffed that her dog's breed had been so honoured. Chuffed? Lara was ecstatic—Idaho was Frida's father. So that confirmed it: she was a blue blood, a veritable princess, a cut above the mainstream mongrels and bitzers.

Of course, none of this matters to the dogs, who run a generally classless society at the park, an equitable

FRIDA THE BERNESE
MOUNTAIN DOG.

utopian arrangement, although I sense Cooper has always considered himself king.

We have also been graced by celebrity—Billy the wheaten terrier was a silver screen star. One day, while Billy and his owner walked along Lyall Bay beach, a movie person with an American accent approached them. 'What a cute dog,' he said, then signed Billy up to be one of the motion-capture dogs for Snowy in Peter Jackson's movie *The Adventures of Tintin*. In the same way that actor Andy Serkis inhabited the character of Gollum in the Lord of the Rings films, so Billy became Snowy.

In preparation for filming, he had to wear an all-encompassing black outfit around home that went down to his paws and just had holes for his head and tail. The idea was for him to get used to it so he wouldn't try to chew it off when they wanted to film him. For the cameras, they put special Velcro dots all over him to sense his movements, and made him walk around and up and down stairs a lot. There was some small payment—enough for a new kennel—and a credit at the movie's end. 'Snowy: Billy', or some such. Billy's movie career seems to have ended after this and I don't think he was ever seen on screen again, nor, sadly, at our dog park.

DESPITE BEING THE MOST POPULAR dogs in New Zealand, we only have a couple of Labradors among the

Tanera dog park regulars. Both are giants, but Louis is marginally huger, a lumbering black cloud of flat fur, an approaching southerly storm of a dog, 40 kilograms of ambling amiability. Named after Louis Armstrong, his size is a fusion of genetics and gluttony. In Louis's world, most things are definable as food: if it fits in his mouth, then it's food. This has included a bottle of orange nail polish scarfed from the bedroom floor of one of the kids at his home. We know this not because anyone saw Louis eat it, but because, having passed largely unaltered through his intestines, it was deposited in the middle of the path in Central Park one morning.

An Easter egg, foil and all, was eaten one year, without any apparent complications. As a puppy, Louis destroyed the family's trampoline, first eating the safety netting surrounding it, then the padding between the springs, rendering it completely unusable.

He also possesses an unerring skill for sensing and seeking out food. His owner, Matthew, arrived one morning with news that Louis had suddenly hived off into the bushes earlier on his walk and returned triumphantly with a pie, still cellophane-wrapped, gently cradled in his gob. 'Steak and cheese,' Matthew reported. 'Lovely.'

Another time, Matthew and the rest of the family were sitting at the back of their house and noticed Louis enthralled in devouring something. It turned out to be a casserole that had been frozen in a large yoghurt container.

The best bet is that a neighbour had left it outside to thaw, and Louis had swung by and figured it was fair game.

Louis's weakness for food is perhaps only matched by his frailty for bitches. When he falls in love with one, he falls hard, trotting after her with his nose mere inches from her rear, his head, which is the size of a breeze block, enveloped in a mask of dreaminess. Matthew tries discipline. 'Louis, get outside!' he shouts. That's one of my favourite dog park commands. But by this stage Louis is well past listening or decorum and trips by almost affixed to the target of his love.

One day it was Aggie, a standard poodle with the gait of a gazelle—a factor which made it difficult for Louis to keep up with her. Occasionally, when she slowed, Louis would almost get within touching distance and you could see his angle shifting slightly, the leg being readied for that half leap on to her rear end. But then she'd be off again, leaving an exasperated Louis trailing. However, at some point Aggie collided with a fox terrier who was digging a trench in the ground, and a split second of ferocity erupted between them. That was all it took. In the instant Aggie was scrapping with the foxie at one end, Louis was in at the other in a disgraceful display of opportunism. Love and war coincided, a collision of dog park extremes, until Matthew arrived and told Louis to get outside.

But 40 kilograms of intent can be valuable. One evening, Matthew was heading home with mates and stopped in at the Brooklyn pub for a nightcap. He'd just got his beer when his wife, Ange, phoned, worried because there was a prowler on their property—the second time it had happened recently. The beer was left unsipped, as Matthew sprinted the 500 metres home, charged with adrenaline and the desire to punch the intruder. But, by the time he arrived, the job had been done. Ange had let Louis out, Louis had barked something an octave below what humans can manage, and the prowler had disappeared.

That's the thing with dogs. Even if they're complete softies, all it takes is a gruff bark or two and a burglar will have second thoughts. Burglars generally can't tell if a dog's growl is one of anxiety or aggression. And, given their occupation, they're unlikely to hang around to work this out. Easier to scout the house next door where the cat lives. So Louis, a danger only to himself in the normal course of a day, is worth every cent it takes to preserve his bulk and bark.

Matthew recounted a wonderful story of meeting a woman at the dog park one afternoon who had a Labrador similar to Louis. The woman, it turned out, was blind and the Lab was her guide dog, and while she and Matthew chatted, their dogs jumped about and chased each other. When it was time to go, the woman started to arrange the harness back on her dog.

'Ah, I don't think that's a good idea,' said Matthew.

The woman, slightly taken aback, stressed that the Lab was her guide dog.

'Yeah, but you've got the wrong Lab,' Matthew replied, pointing out that she was saddling up Louis.

The woman laughed, which is not what she might have been doing if she'd relied on big Lou for assistance. In all probability, instead of getting home she would have had a deluxe tour of Brooklyn's rubbish bins and best-known lairs of abandoned pies.

BRYN THE CORGI WOULD HAVE known a few of these spots. When he first arrived at the park, he was a monster, beyond obese, a blimp somehow supported on four barely visible legs. He wasn't designed to be scrawny or gaunt, but there was no excuse for what had happened to Bryn. He had been fed to near-death by a previous owner, whether out of misguided kindness or contemptible laziness, and had swollen to mammothness.

His new owners, Brent and Pip, had taken in Bryn and taken on the challenge of transforming him, which essentially meant halving his weight. It was the stuff of reality TV shows. Over the months, they succeeded, and Bryn shrank from a sad, stumbling lump of canine corpulence to a cheery, trotting dog with a waist. It was such a happy story, and when Pip and her family turned up at the dog park's Christmas breakfast, it seemed Bryn's life was secure with his new family.

But fate is fickle and unfair and the last chapter of Bryn's life wasn't a happy one. When he developed a tumour after only a year or two with his new family, he stopped eating entirely—an irony we decorously didn't mention much. Before long, Bryn had to be put down. When Brent met Ceri one day and recounted what had happened, he told her to make the most of every day with her dog. She went straight home and gave her labradoodle, Leo, an enormous cuddle.

Pip is a writer, and in 2018 won the country's top literary award for her novel *The New Animals*. It was set in Auckland, involved the fashion world, and had nothing to do with dogs. But every time I heard about Pip's success I liked to think of Bryn, who indeed became a new animal thanks to Pip and her family. For a short time, they gave him the life he was meant to have.

HARRY WAS BORN INTO a life of luxury and affection, but one with considerable realism. Despite loving him dearly and ministering to most of his desires, Barbro is relatively phlegmatic about his character. 'He's not very smart, but he's cunning.'

To verify this, she mentions how, when they return home from the dog park in the morning, she gives Harry and their other dog, Katie, bones—neck bones that she gets especially from the butcher. Harry sets to with his and finishes it up, while Katie occasionally licks and sits and guards and gloats over hers, with an 'Oh, you've finished yours? I've still got mine!' manner. And of course, this is just impossible provocation and temptation for Harry, who eventually reaches his limit. After long moments of staring at Katie's barely touched bone, he will leap up and rush to the front door, barking his head off as if a visitor has arrived and rung the bell. Katie hasn't heard the bell—because it's all a calculated invention by Harry—but she joins in with the yapping scramble to the door. The moment she leaves her bone unattended, Harry quickly doubles back, snaffles it, and whisks it away. The ploy apparently works every time, with Katie ever so slow to learn the ruse.

Then there was the time Harry filched the entire block of lard Barbro had placed in a tree to attract wax-eyes. That only added to Barbro's concerns about his calorific intake, growing girth and associated lack of energy at the dog park. 'He's a little bit inert,' she said one day, as Harry sat observing rather than scampering.

But bones, those bits of anatomy he anticipates so eagerly and prizes so dearly, have also caused inconvenience and expense. One time, Barbro and Ross noted their toilet was blocked and called in the plumber. The plumber's name was Mr Cobra. Well, his business was Cobra Drain Cleaning and Plumbing, but Barbro abridged that and simply referred to him as Mr Cobra. His motto, painted on the back of his van, was 'Our business is in the shit' and the company owed its name to the long black exploratory hose-cum-pipe that goes up drains and discovers the problem. At first, Mr Cobra suspected the blockage might be an invading tree root somewhere downstream, but then the true cause was revealed: one of Harry's bones, wedged fast in the S-bend.

Barbro explained that Harry always tried to sneak his bones inside and she was constantly shooing him out, but this time he must have eluded her defences. Quite why he had decided the toilet was the best place to hide the bone, or how it wasn't noticed before it got flushed and jammed, has never been dwelt on. Maybe Harry was driven by something innate or primal about stashing food. Maybe it was just inexplicable weirdness.

I once met a guy at the park who recounted how he had treated his dog to a cannon bone—one of those giant cow leg bones you'll sometimes find in the dog roll section at the supermarket—which he had got the butcher to saw into three bits. His dog was in heaven, and chewed on the first section for hours. But when the guy went to bed, he found the repellent saliva-coated remains carefully hidden under his pillow. Nope, he never worked out why, either.

Back at Harry's house, the immediate reality was how to dislodge the bone from the toilet's workings. Despite his promises and gadgetry, Mr Cobra couldn't solve the problem. He had to call in a second plumber with a dull name but sharper tools who removed the entire toilet from its base to free the bone and charged $124. Together with Mr Cobra's bill, the offending piece of cow carcass became known as the $300 bone.

Meanwhile, Harry's reputation as both gormless and shrewd was further burnished and bolstered.

5.

The ways we train them

Not all dogs are smart. We've just got to face that. Just as not every human is going to be Stephen Hawking clever, not every dog is going to be Lassie. Consequently, some people might perish down a mineshaft for want of a dog like Lassie being in the vicinity and able to rescue them. But there are ways to make your dog a fraction more obedient, if not a mastermind or virtuoso wonder-dog.

The first family dog we had, a cocker spaniel called Sandy, was genial, but not a Rhodes Scholar, it would be fair to say. Affable, affectionate, not the type to cause trouble, but just not that mentally adroit. So much so that my father nicknamed him Goofy. I think there was also mention of Dopey on occasions.

When Sandy died and we got Gyp, Mum and I thought it would be a good idea to take him to canine obedience classes. Well, I'm imagining Mum suggested it, and I got the job of turning up every Sunday morning on the banks of Blenheim's Taylor River for six weeks of instruction—I can't imagine my teenage self otherwise volunteering to get out of bed early on weekends. Note how they called it canine obedience. That was the aim. Basic control—sit, come, heel—not tricks or show pony agility stuff. It was exactly what we needed.

The idea of going to classes followed a string of nights spent trying to get Gyp to come inside when we just wanted to go to bed but he had other moonlit desires. I remember laying a trail of dog biscuits from our yard to the back door, and then into the kitchen. I'd wait behind the door till Gyp scoffed his way inside, and then swiftly slam it shut behind him. But this was always an emergency measure, and completely the wrong approach—Gyp just saw it as a supplementary feast every evening, and was entirely happy to play his part in the ritual and for it to be repeated daily. Mum probably saw obedience classes as a cheaper alternative to a fortune spent on biscuits to lure Gyp indoors.

In truth—or in my fond memory—Gyp was pretty easy to control, the bits of Border collie we discerned in him having given him a head start in the intelligence stakes. So much so that, with a bit of practice in the evenings, he was soon the class star at obedience school.

Every course ends with a test, where all the dogs are put through their paces, supposedly exuding newly found obedience. It is, of course, a stage for glory or humiliation.

At week five of our course, we were informed that the top dog at next week's examination would win a bag of Tux dog biscuits. Not some silly snack pack, but a 20-kilogram whopper.

I knew about these things because the previous year I'd worked at the local Tux factory on weekends and after school, earning money for a college cricket trip to Australia. I swept floors, I made up cardboard boxes, but mostly I packed biscuits. These triangular staples of New Zealand dogs' diet would arrive along a conveyer belt from some other part of the factory, fresh and redolent, and our job was to fill boxes and sacks with them, then stack these on a pallet. It was simple work, and it was tedious.

Simple, tedious work breeds foolishness to disrupt the monotony. So it was that one Saturday morning it was decided we should taste the biscuits to see what they were like. It wasn't a dare, or punishment for losing a bet—we were just bored and curious and the biscuits were still warm. I can't remember the exact flavour—somewhere between sawdust and sausages, I imagine—but I do remember we were all mildly surprised at how palatable they were. A bit dry, but nothing a knob of butter wouldn't have fixed. Snacking on Tux biscuits didn't become a fixture at the factory, though—there were Milk Arrowroots and Super Wines in the smoko room. And by the time we got Gyp, I had another job, working on a milk round.

But I knew the value of a 20-kilogram bag of Tux

biscuits, knew how much Gyp liked them, knew what a saving it would be. And, aged fifteen, I had a competitive streak, an ego that needed bolstering and a black-and-white mongrel I'd fast become devoted to. In a class of largely pedigree dogs, Gyp was the 'mixed breed', like the kid from some provincial college among prefects from private schools. So we practised harder than ever in that last week, till the drills were instinctive, the response to directions instantaneous.

I can remember only a couple of things from that final obedience class: Gyp disgracing himself, and my mortification as someone else swanned off with the sack of Tux.

It had all come down to the final exercise, the one where you had to show your dog would stay when you told it to, and come when instructed. You all lined up, dogs at your side, and one by one you told your dog to stay while you walked out a dozen or so paces. Then, you turned and called your dog with the simple command 'come'. They were meant to race straight to you, circle behind, then sit at your side, looking up with adoring anticipation for the next order. Gyp and I had done this a hundred times, we'd done it until we were both bored, but we'd never done it with a bitch on heat just along the line.

Now, what someone was doing bringing a dog on heat to an obedience class is beyond me, but it was always destined to end in disaster—and that's surely what unravelled.

When it was my turn, Gyp dutifully sat still when I told him to stay and walked away from him, then stopped and turned around. But, when I called him to come, he hesitated, glanced down the line, came forward two paces then commenced a wide arc that bent away from me and towards the temptress. He was caught between obedience and lust, conscience and opportunity. Lust and opportunity, as ever, triumphed, until he completed a neat semi-circle, was facing away from me and had his nose inches from the bitch.

I imagine there was sniggering from the others in the class. I know there was scowling from the judges. And I know it broke my adolescent heart not to win that bag of biscuits. We'd been so good until then. We'd been robbed. And Gyp's one shot to stand atop a podium had disappeared, vanishing on a hormonal whim.

I took him home in silence.

I probably gave him a biscuit when we got there.

MY NEXT BRUSH WITH CANINE obedience came nearly 20 years later, but ended much the same way. By the time we got Cas, I was back in Marlborough and classes were now being held at the A&P showgrounds on a weeknight. And by now, there were things called puppy preschool, gatherings of fluffballs perched on their owners' laps or hiding under chairs, that were meant to be all about socialisation and getting a few basics sorted. So we'd taken Cas to that before enrolling her in obedience classes, confident she was a natural-born genius because she'd come from a farm and farm dogs are the best at obedience and obeisance.

Cas, it turned out, was a delinquent, initially at least. She was still a pup, and an hour of lessons was just too much. After 30 minutes, she'd start squirming and trying to take off, and there was little hope of getting her to do anything useful. But, gradually, she got it. We'd practise our skills daily at the dog park, and towards the end of the course she was top of the class. At least, I thought so.

But once again, there was a test, a final parade of diligence, a court of how well you and your dog had learned your lessons. And sitting in judgment was a woman called Betty, the mother of a work colleague, who had some important and badged role in the local dog club. I didn't really know Betty and expected no favours— which was good, because she gave none. Instead, she gave Cas scores ranging from miserable to middling for the various disciplines—temperament, sitting, heeling, coming, et cetera. I'll admit, the heel had been a little ropey, with Cas tugging a fraction too much and my fast walk nearly becoming a jog in order to keep up with her and give the impression the lead was suitably slack and we were side by side. However, the rest was flawless, I thought. Betty didn't.

When the final results were tallied and the certificates handed out in descending order of placings, I stood empty and slightly disbelieving as I waited for our names to be announced. By the time they got to us, midfield, I was feeling wretched that I'd let Cas down and embarrassed her with my poor performance.

There was no bag of Tux at stake this time, thank goodness, but the car trip home was just as silent and glum as it had been all those years earlier with Gyp.

DOUBLY BRUISED, AND DESPITE NEVER really getting over my failures with Gyp and Cas, I didn't think twice about taking Cooper to obedience school when we got him. In truth, any final test was peripheral, largely meaningless, a subjective appraisal from a hobbyist. The true value of the courses was how they transformed unruly pups into dogs who mostly did what they were told.

Just mastering the basics of sit and stay and come can make life with any dog so much happier and safer. More advanced skills, such as getting them to heel, can convert your walks from ill-tempered arm-wrenching trials to pleasurable meanders. It is such a small investment at the beginning of your time with your dog that will provide rewards as long as you're together. Any argument that you're too busy is selfish folly. Any assumption your dog is already clever enough is likely delusion also.

On a drizzly Sunday morning two months after we got Cooper, I tried to restrain him as he hauled me up the dog-legged path to the Central Allbreeds Dog Training School in Wellington's shadowed Aro Valley for our first lesson. All the dog owners stood waiting for the instructor, with the normal exchange of perfunctory introductions and muted conversation. The dogs, however, were rioting. So much fun. So many new friends. The smells of a thousand dogs who had pissed on the AstroTurf during past courses. This place was awesome!

There was a clubhouse with carpet the colour of gold and vomit, couches with foam gnawed by bored puppies, a table with a sandwich-maker, and copies of *Two Cats One Dog* magazine and *New Zealand Dog World*. The latest issue of the club's newsletter, *Lamppost*, was pinned to the noticeboard. On the walls were lists of Canine Good Citizens with merit, bronze, silver and gold awards, a pink-and-white sash from the 1984 national dog show, and a list of the club's Life Members. Ringing two sides of the room were faded photos of champion dogs, predominantly brainbox Border collies, but there was also a big poodle, something that could have been a Hungarian vizsla and maybe a Lab. The picture of the Border collie leaping through a flaming hoop was the real standout though.

Our class of ten was the predictable all-breed allsorts. There was a cute twelve-week-old husky, a big tan thing of unknown derivation called Jack, Massey the giant mastiff, tiny Tucker (who wanted to hump Massey really badly), Doozer, who refused to go outside if it was wet, and Ralph, a brindle Staffie with a streak of greyhound.

Ralph had been hit by a car when young, lost a back leg and been given up to the SPCA by his owners, from where he was rescued by teenaged Esther and her family. It was great to see Esther taking responsibility for their dog—often it's kids who plead for a puppy and make extravagant promises about walking it, but then the parents end up doing everything. Esther sort of reminded me of myself when I was training Gyp—minus the dyed hair and bone carving around her neck. You wouldn't have got far with those in Blenheim in 1979.

And then there was Pip. We'd seen Pip at the SPCA when we had been searching for a dog. She was a one-year-old huntaway and looked just what we were after—sleek and shiny and smart—but there was a note tied to her cage saying she was already taken. We stood looking through the grille at Pip and wished we'd come a few days earlier. However, the next time we visited the SPCA, we found Cooper and quickly forgot about Pip.

But when we started going to Tawatawa dog park, there was Pip with her new owners, Cheryl and Steve. And she was manic. Particularly with Cooper. A bully, even. She'd circle Cooper, barking and goading him, and he would snap and shrink and struggle to know what was going on. It was about then, and after Cheryl said Pip had chewed through the main computer cable at her work, that we secretly thanked fate we'd missed out on her. And the same thing happened at obedience classes, Pip trying to dominate Cooper, and none of us really understanding why. The strangest thing is that now, nearly ten years on, whenever Cooper sees Pip at the dog park, he can't keep away from her. His tail and ears will perk up and he'll dance around, wanting to play, trying to impress her as if she's the greatest dog in the world. Pip doesn't bully or bark at him any more; she just largely ignores him and trots off. I guess it's domination of a different kind, with Cooper still not understanding quite what he's done wrong or why Pip still doesn't love him.

Back on the fake grass of the Central Allbreeds club, instructors Karen and Kate and Shelley spent eight weeks training us how to train our dogs to sit and wait and stay and come and lie down and not jump. How they should be placid when a stranger or another dog came to greet them, how to let someone run their hands all over them and check their mouth and ears and paws—vital during vet examinations. And underpinning everything was the importance of positive reinforcement rather than punishment: a limitless supply of treats to reward good behaviour rather than reprimanding bad behaviour with a raised voice or hand, or worse. The instructors also used one of those clicker things that are supposed to make communication and cooperation between you and your dog a cinch, but Cooper never really got it and the noise drove me nuts. After each hour-long lesson, the dogs would be let off and go wild, rarking around as a pack, doing laps of the clubhouse, tumbling and tussling together.

The final day was, again, test time, the prospect of which I was now loathing. The week before, Cooper had leaped all over the instructor during a meet-and-greet, cordiality overcoming his calm. But on exam day he went through his paces pretty perfectly. I thought he was the best all round, but they didn't score anyone. In fact, they did their darndest to pass everyone—even the ones who failed miserably at certain disciplines. Like Sunny the little white poodle, who wouldn't know a 'come' from a cornfield in Nebraska. She had no idea what she was meant to do and just sat beside the instructor, bemused, lead limp, while her owner, ten metres away, called and danced and whistled and sashayed from side to side to get her attention and Sunny stayed rooted, staring elsewhere. They gave Sunny a separate test later on, where the distance required to come was reduced to something barely beyond arm's length, and somehow convinced themselves she understood what the command meant.

Jack wasn't too crash hot on coming, either. In the test, you had to call your dog and they had to run to you through a gauntlet of the other dogs. Jack got three-quarters of the way towards his owner, Richard, and everything was looking good as he sped past the rest of us, lead flying out behind him. Then, we watched a sickening curve begin—the sort that starts as a small deviation that alarms the owner, and quickly becomes a full-scale, disaster-spelling handbrake turn.

So, while Jack roared off into the wings to sniff the other dogs, Richard kept calling him insistently. Jack looked up, started back towards Richard, and then there was that split second when you could see Jack weighing up his options: Do I go to my owner, who I spend all day with and who makes me do dumb shit I don't really want to do? Or, do I run unshackled, like a wolf in the wild, and play with my new buddies?

They say that dogs just want to please you. In my experience, there's an element of truth in that—but, generally, this happens only when what you want them to do coincides with what they've already got in mind. In the main, dogs just want to do what pleases *them*, and tend to turn deaf and blind when you counter that with bellowed commands. The image of dewy-eyed devotion from dogs towards their owners can't be denied, but it's undermined by myriad examples of exasperated owners shouting into the ether for Rover to come back/stop rolling in that filth/leave the other dog alone/get out of the rubbish. In this revised and more realistic picture, Rover is usually having far too much fun for the concept of pleasing his master to enter his calculations.

So it was that, as Jack stood there considering whether

to obey Richard or run free with his mates, freedom won, and Jack returned to the other dogs for more play, until he was collared. He eventually passed a more private test.

Massey also tested the generosity of those judging him. The instructor and her dog had barely arrived in front of Massey for a meet-and-greet, when Massey lunged forward frothing, all quivering jowls that seemed to say, 'fresh meat, fresh meat', front legs suspended in the air as his owner hauled him back using the doubled-up climbing rope that served as his lead. A rapid distraction by way of treats made it seem he was under control, and Massey was given a pass. Later, he somehow got away, breaking the carabiner between his collar and lead. 'Loose dog! Loose dog!' cried an instructor, as Massey revelled in brief freedom.

So, in the end, all the misfits and miscreants received a certificate attesting to their obedience. Obedience is a broad term at times like this, it seems.

Despite no one having been ranked, as we drove home I told Cooper he was the best, as I often did. I slipped his certificate into a drawer, and fetched a bigger-than-usual bone from the fridge for his lunch.

THE WHOLE IDEA OF TRAINING by reward makes sense. But, occasionally, there seems scope for instant reprimand or a slightly tougher approach. This can take all manner of forms. Some people say you should carry a bottle of water with you on walks and squirt your dog whenever they err or offend. A variation of that is spraying them with citronella, which supposedly dogs hate. You can get citronella collars that shoot a jet at them every time they bark if that's what you're trying to cure. And then there are the controversial shock collars, through which a brief electrical pulse can be sent whenever the dog does something bad.

Shock collars seem evil and, while there are calls for them to be outlawed, others swear by them. One of them is Jim Pottinger, who runs what they call kiwi aversion or avoidance courses. Essentially, it's training dogs to never go near, let alone attack, kiwi or other native species, such as penguins. Some areas around the country require you to have done these courses before you can take your dog into the bush. The Remutaka Forest near Wainuiomata is one of them, and, because we wanted to go walking there, we signed Cooper up for one of Jim's courses. It was something of a revelation.

Jim buckled a thick shock collar around Cooper's neck, and off we went to a circuit Jim had prepared in a small patch of bush. Around this were six points where he had laid what resembled kiwi carcasses, which carried the birds' scent. At one location, there was also a model kiwi, which popped up as you walked past while a nearby speaker sent out a kiwi's call.

Standing beside Jim, I let Cooper off the lead and he did

what he always does, trotting confidently ahead of me. At the first kiwi, Cooper caught its scent and stopped, edging over to it and dropping his nose till it almost touched the bird. At that instant, Jim sent a short shock through Cooper's collar via a controller he was holding. I have a very clear memory of Cooper yelping and somehow flying backwards, all four legs off the ground, and landing about a metre away. At the next bird, Cooper showed interest and headed towards it. This time, Jim gave him a reduced shock and Cooper immediately backed away.

What followed was as clear a vindication of the method as you could get. At each of the next checkpoints, Cooper refused to go near the bird. Instead, he made a large semicircular diversion through the undergrowth to avoid it. Jim was happy. I was amazed. The whole thing had taken ten minutes and two fleeting shocks, and had taught Cooper to associate the smell and sound of a kiwi with something nasty.

Jim said, 'Come back in a year, and we'll see if this connection is still imprinted on his brain.' So we did, and it was stunning to see the effect of that initial training. Every time Cooper caught wind of the kiwi, he diverted far away from it, before rejoining the path, not wanting to go anywhere near the birds. Jim never once touched the shock controller. This time Jim said, 'Come back in two years.' Again, we did, and the results were exactly the same.

So now, when we go tramping, we do so in confidence

that Cooper is no danger to kiwi. It might be considered tantamount to cruelty by some, and there may be other methods, but it seems a small and very brief price to pay for such a worthy end.

AFTER COOPER FINISHED THE FIRST round of obedience classes at Central Allbreeds , we carried on to grade two, dubbed 'Practical Canine'. This was essentially the same as grade one, but was conducted in a public place with more people and potential distractions. Our classes were held on Wellington's waterfront.

We did 'recall training' (which is when you call your dog to you) on a grassy area beside Te Papa where, at night, the homeless and drunk sheltered among the surrounding flax bushes. On a sunny Sunday morning as we gathered, the smell of dope smoke drifted from the same shrubbery. Somebody trying to make the perfect day just a bit better, I guessed. None of the dogs cared and none of them showed a Lassie-like inclination to rush into the bushes, make a citizen's arrest and get a pat from a policeman.

There were, however, plenty of other things to distract our dogs from their tasks: rollerbladers and prams and bikes and ducks, and bacon smells from cafes, and kids struggling with fast-melting ice creams. A whole lot was going on, but all the dogs navigated their way through the maze of temptations and emerged with another certificate.

Obedience classes are one thing. They're ideal for instilling the fundamentals, perfect for moulding a controllable dog. But learning other things can be a lottery, although the basics of rewarding good behaviour and not giving your dog a bollocking for failure remain. Take teaching a dog to swim. How do you do that? In my experience, you don't. They'll come to it when they're ready, and some may never be truly ready. From the front deck of our house, I've watched people over on the beach simply wade into the water cradling their dogs in their arms, and dump them out of their depth. The assumption is that the dog will have to instantly learn to swim. But I've frequently seen them instantly panic and flail and splutter their way back to the beach and then run away from their owners. So I'm not persuaded the blunt sink-or-swim approach works, but can't offer any sure-fire alternatives.

I'm sure there are some. The internet is awash with dog whisperers, canine maharishis who will tell you that training a dog is straightforward, and promise a household radiating human–dog Zen. From Barbara Woodhouse to Cesar Millan to a guy called Doggy Dan in Auckland, it's all there in confident video clips. They dress as if they're going on safari, they promise golden rules, they encourage you to sign up for newsletters. And sometimes, they'll have the answer you're looking for. But, when it comes to training dogs, I'm not convinced anybody has all the answers. Your best bet is just a lot of love and patience.

6.
The heartache
they cause us

BEWARE of the DOG

ONE DAY IT WILL RIP YOUR BEATING
HEART FROM YOUR CHEST & BREAK
IT IN TWO.

I guess the one thing I'm really grateful for is that I didn't hear him being hit. Or, god forbid, see it happen. All I saw was Hobbs's grey backside disappearing gracefully as he hurdled our front gate and dashed across the road. I was on the phone to Nikki when I saw him escape, told her 'gotta go', slammed down the phone and raced out the door and through the gate. By the time I reached the pavement—at most ten seconds after seeing Hobbs bolt—he'd been hit by a passing car.

It was December 2011 and Hobbs was coming up to his second birthday that Christmas Eve. We'd met Hobbs, a sleek slate-coloured Border collie–German short-haired pointer cross, and his owners, Jan and Briar, at the dog park soon after we got Cooper and had quickly became good friends, and likewise the dogs. Since I worked from home, I'd often look after Hobbs during the day. Cooper and Hobbs would snuggle into the same basket when they were small, or sun themselves on our front deck, keeping each other happy company until it was time for their afternoon walk. In over a year of this routine, Hobbs had never shown any sign he'd jump the front gate, which was about a metre high. But, in a way, I should have foreseen what might happen.

I don't know whether it's an actual psychological condition, but, without doubt, Hobbs has an obsession with balls. Anyone with a ball-thrower has the same effect on him as a butcher lobbing sausages would have on most dogs. Reason becomes a distant planet at such times, obedience a galaxy far, far away. And when a dog is in that space, they can't hear you scream.

Two days earlier, when Jan arrived back at our place after taking the dogs for their afternoon walk, Hobbs had spied our friend Linda throwing balls for her dogs, Pipi and Kelly, over the road on the beach. As Jan opened the car's hatch, Hobbs had leaped out and streaked across to the beach to join them, followed by Cooper. The same thing happened the next day, though thankfully this time Cooper stayed put. But, for Hobbs, the excited barks of dogs he knew, the lure of the beach and, above all, the sight of balls being thrown were all too much, and any drilled-in road sense was jettisoned in the blind pursuit of fun.

And so it was this day. From the front deck at our place, Hobbs had slivers of the view across the road to the beach. Just before midday, Linda, ball-thrower raised, had walked into Hobbs's line of sight, with Pipi and Kelly sprinting along the sand. It sounds trite, but it really did happen in a split second. As I slammed the phone down and raced after Hobbs, I was just hoping like hell I'd see him bounding along the beach to greet Linda. But he didn't make it across.

While I'm forever thankful I was spared the sound of the impact, I've never been able to stop recalling that sickening first sight of him sprawled across the road on his side. All I could think was, *Oh, god, he's not moving. If he's not dead, he soon will be, and I'm going to have to watch him gasp his last few breaths.*

When I reached Hobbs, he was whimpering, with piss coming from his rear end and blood coming from his mouth, staining the asphalt. The car that had hit him was backing up, and people were getting out. The driver and passenger—two guys in their twenties with cropped hair—jogged up and said, so sorry, man, the dog just raced out in front of them, they didn't have a chance to stop. And it's true. Hobbs had cut out from between our parked car and a neighbour's vehicle, giving them no chance to brake in time. It was never their fault, but at that moment I couldn't spend much time reassuring them. Swamped with shock and deserted by the calm decision-making required in such circumstances, I instantly bent down and picked up Hobbs, as he tried to rear up and moaned loudly. When the car's passenger offered to help, Hobbs rounded on him and tried to bite him.

As I stood there in the middle of the road with a dying dog in my arms, my mind whirled about what to do. I knew I needed to get him to a vet immediately if he was going to have any chance—but how? I went to put him in our car, but the door was locked, so I asked the other car's passenger to quickly get the keys out of my pocket. When he eventually did this, he couldn't work out how to unlock the damn door. So I desperately asked them if they could take me to the vet, but they said sorry, they had kids with them and had to be somewhere.

And then an angel arrived. I use that word reluctantly, given I have no belief in fate or the supernatural. But there's little other way to describe her and the remarkable timing of her intercession. Her name was Monique, a detail I didn't discover till later as we raced to the vet. All I knew at that instant was that, as I stood cradling a fast-fading Hobbs and wondering what to do, a woman appeared over my shoulder. 'I'm an SPCA vet nurse,' she said. 'Can I help?' I still have no idea where she was going or what she thought was going on. Whatever her plans were, she abandoned them and became the answer to my panicking quandary.

She said she could take us to the vet, so I jumped into her car with Hobbs. Then she asked if I wanted to lock up my house first and I realised Cooper was still there, with the gate wide open. So I slid Hobbs across the gear lever and handbrake and handed him to Monique, then raced back through the gate and put a bemused and slightly frightened Cooper inside, slamming the door behind me. Back in Monique's car, I took Hobbs on to my lap again, but couldn't get the bloody seatbelt done up so, as we took off, the alarm was pinging madly, only adding to the cacophony and confusion, until I worked out how to make the belt click with one hand.

Hobbs was breathing rapidly, and Monique said he needed pain relief. 'Which vet do you want to go to?' she asked. Island Bay's vet was the closest, and Monique said we could also go to the SPCA in Newtown, which wasn't too much further, but I decided to head to Central Vets, about six kilometres away at the bottom of Brooklyn Hill, because it was where Hobbs went and they called themselves a hospital. Looking back, I wonder why I didn't take up Monique's suggestion to go to the SPCA, where they're well set up for emergencies and she could have directed everything. But at the time I was just focused on the idea of getting Hobbs to his regular vet for some reason—a reasonably non-vital fixation that gives me concern for my decision-making abilities should I ever be in, say, a plane crash, a high-rise inferno or a terrorist attack in a shopping mall.

Monique had only been living in Wellington for three weeks and had no idea where she was heading.

'Just drive,' I said. 'I'll tell you where to go.'

'Shall we go fast?' she asked.

'Yes,' I said.

So, all up Happy Valley Road and Ohiro Road, we sped past cars and I hoped they'd understand it was an emergency and wouldn't *555 us. On the way down Brooklyn Hill, we got stuck behind a slow ute and the driver obviously thought we were being bogan wankers so he braked and we almost rear-ended him, forcing us to pull back and fret. Along the way, I'd managed to pull out my phone and ring Jan—who, as it happened, had just sat down to lunch with Briar in Seatoun. I told her briefly what had happened and where we were going.

'Oh, my god,' she said, and told me she'd be there as soon as she could.

At the vet clinic, Monique and I swung into the parking space and two nurses inside looked up from the reception counter to see Hobbs in my arms and me motioning for them to open the doors. They pointed me down a corridor and into a room where I laid Hobbs on a stainless steel table. Everyone else was calm. I was sick. A vet arrived and started checking Hobbs over, then they shaved a patch of fur off his leg to put in an intravenous line for pain relief and fluids. The colour around his gums was pallid. As I stood beside the cold steel table, I imagine my face was equally drained of colour.

Jan arrived and tearfully crept up the corridor to join me. 'Is he all right?'

I didn't want to answer her, because the answer was 'yes and no'. He was still alive, and that was a really good thing.

But who knew what was going on inside him?

Briar arrived. Then more vets came to help.

After about fifteen minutes, they suggested we go out to the waiting room while they did X-rays and other tests, and at this point, Monique the angel excused herself. Briar, who seemed remarkably positive, asked me how I was doing. I looked down at my bare feet and mumbled something about not being brilliant but not as bad as them, I guessed. What I really felt was an incredible sense of guilt for this all happening when I was looking after their dog.

Eventually, the vet came out to tell us they couldn't see any breakages but there wasn't any response in Hobbs's right front leg. She explained this was a common injury in car-versus-dog cases, and often resulted in amputation as all the nerves were ripped away by the impact. It would just be a matter of waiting and seeing how he coped over the next 24 hours or so, she said.

I left Jan and Briar to wait with Hobbs, and caught a taxi home. When I got there, the front door was open and Cooper was gone. I panicked, thinking he had also jumped the gate and disappeared. Two dogs in one day. But no—I realised that in my haste to get Hobbs to the vet, I had slammed the door behind me a bit violently and it had bounced back open, and Cooper had simply wandered out onto the back deck to snooze in the sun. He was okay.

Only one dog disaster to dwell on.

NIKKI AND I WENT BACK to the vet's later that evening, and Hobbs was lying in a foam cradle in a back room, hooked up to a drip, Briar bleary-eyed and sitting on the floor beside him. He had a blanket over him and, when he saw us come in, it began lifting and falling as his tail wagged under it. It was the best possible thing to see, and gave me hope he was going to make it. He was still breathing fast and not really able to move, but everyone seemed positive about the outcome.

By this time, word about Hobbs's accident had got around the dog park contingent, and Barbro had already popped down to the vet clinic to check on him and on Briar and Jan. Barbro was amazed at how enthusiastically Hobbs responded to her, despite obviously feeling miserable, and later sent me a text so wise and true that I still frequently reflect on it and repeat it often: 'The "why me?" is for humans.'

Eventually, Nick the vet and I lifted Hobbs out to Briar's car, and they took him to the after-hours vet so he could be watched overnight.

Nikki and I had to go out of town that weekend, and by the time we got back Hobbs was home. The vets were happy for him to be there because Jan and Briar are nurses and understood the drugs and care he needed. When we visited, Hobbs started moaning and his tail wagged in welcome, although he still couldn't move much and had spent the afternoon lying on the lawn hooked up to his drip, with the bag suspended from a tree.

The next day, Jan and Briar took Hobbs to Massey University's vet clinic in Palmerston North for more scans and checks. It became clear that his shoulder had borne the brunt of the impact and the bulk of the damage, the upshot being that his right front leg hung limply, virtually wrenched away from the rest of his body, with no connecting nerves. The vets said they'd wait another six weeks to see if he got movement back in the leg, but if not it would have to be removed.

Jan and Briar had already had a few days to come to terms with this prospect, and really only had one question for the vets: Whatever happens, can Hobbs live a happy and full life? The answer was absolutely, unequivocally yes. So, from that point on, there was nothing but optimism and dealing with the practicalities of getting him better.

THE AMAZING THING, WHICH WE all gradually came to appreciate, is how incredibly fortunate Hobbs actually was. Apart from his leg, he suffered little major damage. His heart was shunted to one side by the impact, causing a partially collapsed lung, but no arteries broke. His pelvis and back legs were okay. There was no spinal damage. No ribs were broken—if one had cracked and gone through his lung, he would have probably died. If the car had hit him 30 centimetres forward of his shoulder, it would have smashed his head and killed him. If it had been 30 centimetres behind his shoulder, it would have ruptured his organs with the same outcome. It could have so easily ended right there on the road outside our house.

So, in hindsight, all you could say was, 'Shit, he was lucky.' Unlucky to have dashed across the road just as a car came along, for sure. But, in the scale of things, so damn lucky to have lived.

Initially, however, even basic movements and the simplest things, like getting him to pee, were difficult. In an effort to help, Cooper would come around and we'd make him pee in the garden and instinctively Hobbs would do the same, in the same spot, as he'd always done. Knowing Hobbs had never been able to resist peeing on road cones, Jan and Briar stole one from some nearby roadworks and put it on their top deck, just through the door from his bed, for him to use. (It was returned when he became more mobile.)

Keeping his damaged leg out of the way was also an issue. It just flopped and dragged and tripped him up—so Jan and Briar got a T-shirt from Kmart that they put over his head and chest, hooking his bad leg up in it, and that worked perfectly.

For the first ten days, Hobbs lay sad and sleepy at home. I'd go around to keep him company, and he'd just lie beside me and prop his head on my leg while Cooper bounced around trying to get him to play ball. Then, one day when

I was there, Jan came home and Hobbs got up and greeted her, then went and found his big green ball and started throwing it at her. His ears were up, and from then on he was sort of back to his old self. Just like that. It was almost instantaneous.

For two months, we lived in hope. Hoping that the nerves around his shoulder would knit. Hoping that he'd miraculously regain mobility in his injured leg. Hoping things would return to how they had been before the accident. None of us really believed in miracles, but right then none of us wanted to deny one might possibly happen.

And Hobbs did get some movement back. He was able to flick his damaged leg forward a bit. I'd watch him when he was fast asleep, chasing rabbits or balls or other dogs in his dreams, and first his claws then his paw and eventually his whole damaged leg would spasm and twitch, and you'd be sure there was progress. And at one of his check-ups, the vet said there were signs of feeling in the pads of his paw. Everyone was very upbeat.

But, as the weeks went by, it became clear his leg was a real encumbrance and he started chewing it, just like the vets had suggested may happen. They can't feel it, or can only feel it a bit, so they don't feel the pain they're causing as they bite it. His paw got sweaty and infected. He ate his way through the leather boots and bandages we put over it to stop his biting, and when we weren't watching he would chew it till the fur was stripped back.

After two months, when Jan and Briar took Hobbs for a check-up, Kerry, the vet they saw most often, tested his reactions and said he hadn't really got back much feeling. Then she told them the leg had to be amputated. When you've spent so long doing everything you can to save your dog's leg and make sure he recovers, it's the news you hate to hear. And, no matter how rational you've been about his prospects, it's still a shock of sorts.

However, the best thing was that the vet made the decision, made it very clearly, and didn't leave it to anyone else to debate or dither. She just firmly told Briar and Jan that it had to come off and made an appointment for three days' time. Everyone knew it was ultimately for the best, but there was something terribly final about it—you can't have second thoughts or change your mind once a limb has been removed.

After the operation, we called around and Hobbs immediately began his moaning in welcome while wagging his tail, despite having 42 stitches in a huge V around his chest. There was no escaping the almost brutal incision, but you had to admire how carefully and cleanly Nick the vet had been in his surgery. It was an incredible job, and one that just capped the phenomenal care the vet clinic had given Hobbs.

Within days, Hobbs was back up and bouncing around on three legs, and the hardest thing was to stop him from popping his stitches and causing internal swelling. Within two months, the fur had grown back and there was this lovely sleek swoop of body where his leg had been. And, of course, he hasn't slowed up at all—well, by a quarter, perhaps. The only difference is that now, when he stands, he forms the typical tripod of an amputee dog, his hind legs spread a bit further apart and his remaining front leg angled in slightly and planted in the centre of his body.

Nick and everyone at the vet clinic were amazed by Hobbs's progress, and remarked on how he was an incredibly tough dog, his recovery aided by being young and fit. Over the past eight years, he has indeed been able to live a full and happy life, just as the Massey vets confirmed that day. The greatest proof of that is when you're at the dog park and Hobbs is racing around with the others, and someone who hasn't seen him before will eventually cry with surprise, 'He's only got three legs!' (Quite often, they actually say, 'He's only got one leg!') It's taken them ten minutes to even notice there's something different, something missing.

Unfortunately, none of this can ever erase the horrid memory of that first sight of Hobbs lying on the road after he'd been hit. I couldn't wait for it to rain and wash the bloodstain off the road outside our house.

I still feel guilty as shit.

And I still wish the gate had been higher to stop him from jumping over it. But it is what it is. And Hobbs is what he is now—slightly physically diminished, but still a fantastic, brilliant, gorgeous dog.

THERE HAVE BEEN TIMES, IN the years since the accident, when we've noticed Hobbs slowing up and let ourselves think that this was the beginning of the end. The reality is that, if a dog is going to lose a leg, it's better for it to be a back one, as there's more weight to support at the front end with their neck and head. We've always known that the physical stress of Hobbs carrying his body around on one less limb would have some effect down the line. We knew arthritis was inevitable. And we knew that if his remaining front leg became weakened there would be little we'd be able to do.

So, you watch for signs and you let your mind get ahead of itself. It's hard not to, sometimes. Some mornings, when I'd pick Hobbs up for a walk, I'd notice his usually invigorated gait from the back doorstep to the car where Cooper waited had become a laboured lurching—each step a deliberate heave. And in the afternoons, going up the hill path, he seemed to crab a lot more, his back legs bunched under him as he hopped along at an angle. Sometimes, he'd try to sprint, as of old, but pull up in pain and whimper a bit.

Jan said the saddest thing was the day he couldn't get to the gate in time to give the postie a rark up. Usually,

Hobbs was alerted to the postie's imminent arrival by the squeaking brakes on his motorbike from a couple of houses up the road. But this time, even though Hobbs set off in advance, the postie had already sped on to the neighbour's by the time Hobbs got to the front gate. Jan said it was heartbreaking to see him peering around the corner, straining to see the postie, his barks echoing after the little red motorbike.

WHAT I'VE REALLY ADMIRED IS the pragmatism and optimism everyone has reacted with. At one stage, Briar and Jan bought Hobbs a harness so they could hold him while he went down stairs and he wouldn't have so much weight on his front paw. They also have a little boot for the paw if the ground is particularly rough. The vets said, 'Yeah, give him painkillers, no problem—there's no point in him being in pain.' So, twice a day, Hobbs has a pill of gabapentin and the effect has been miraculous.

He still has his bad days, days when everything seems stiff and unaligned. But every time we've counted him out and begun counting the days till terminal immobility, we've been amazed at how he's rebounded. Sometimes, as he streaks across the dog park, or relentlessly circles someone with a ball-thrower while barking flat out, or insists on playing with his small rugby ball well past bedtime, you think, *You're a marvel, mate.*

Interestingly, Hobbs isn't the first dog with three legs I've cared for. Or even the second. Years ago, I was living in the Bay of Islands and there were two three-legged dogs in my then-girlfriend's extended family: a hulking German shepherd and a huntaway who'd fallen off the back of a farmer's ute. The huntaway, Queenie, had shattered her leg in the fall and it couldn't be fixed. The farmer wasn't keen on paying for an amputation only to be left with a dog who wasn't much use rounding up sheep, so my girlfriend's sister, who worked at the vet clinic, decided to adopt her.

I'd often take the two amputees walking, and when people passed by they'd notice the first one and coo and pat and whisper sympathy. Then, a few paces on, they'd notice you had another dog missing a leg, and I swear you could see their faces drop and their suspicions rise. The gleam in their eyes became a glare accusing you of being some kind of butcher, some malevolent mistreater of dogs who should be reported and banned from having contact with animals.

The reality, of course, was that it was random coincidence and both dogs were doted on. But, in that instant on the pavement, such explanations were wholly pointless.

I'M NOT SURE EXACTLY WHEN I noticed the small black nodule on Cooper's leg. Right front leg, just above the ankle, around the back. I wish I could remember when it was. Then I might be able to rebuke myself more accurately for how long I'd been aware of it before I went to the vet. And, even then, it was only during Cooper's annual check-up and vaccination that I brought it to the attention of Pete, our vet. It looked like a small blood blister about, oh, the size of half a pea, perhaps. Cooper intermittently gets knocks and scrapes and scars, and I just thought it was something like that—the natural result of an active dog who races after sticks and bounds into blackberry and gorse bushes to fetch them.

It must have been several weeks or, god, perhaps more than a month—time slips by so quickly when corralled by routine—between first noticing it and showing it to Pete. He frowned a bit, said it didn't look like much, but he didn't like the fact it was black. And then he said it might be a melanoma. I'd never even considered that, never even knew dogs got melanoma. How? They have fur covering their skin. But yes, they do get them.

Pete suggested removing the growth and I said, 'Yep.'

'We can do it tomorrow,' Pete said.

I said, 'Yep,' and we booked him in.

Pete said he didn't necessarily think we needed to send it off for histology, but I said, 'Yep, let's do it. We've got pet insurance.'

So, the next day, I left Cooper with the cooing vet nurse, Georgia, in a sheepskin-lined crate to be sedated and operated on. A few nights later, Sally, another vet at the practice who's also Pete's wife, rang to give us the results. It was indeed a melanoma. Then she mentioned some statistics that I don't remember exactly, but didn't seem terribly good. It was something like '15 per cent of dogs with this melanoma live for another year'—or was it two? Afterwards, I wondered if I'd got that bit right, and wished I'd got Sally to spell it out a bit more clearly, though I think I was scared to get her to repeat it. A bit of statistical muddiness can mask hopelessness.

Anyway, the pathologist had said he wasn't sure how badly malignant it was, but the cell division was higher than they'd like. On the up side was the fact the margin they'd cut around the lump was good, and it had come off in one piece, so that was a bonus. Overall, the prognosis was positive, but they just couldn't tell for sure.

I certainly had no way of knowing. I kept positive—but lurking in the background was that line about how only 15 per cent of dogs with this survive.

Sally said we just had to keep an eye on it, watch for other lumps or any changes in pigmentation around where the first lump had been, and check Cooper's lymph nodes under and in front of the affected leg. She said if there was no sign of it returning after six months we could breathe more easily. Fuck. That's a long time to hold your breath. As Nikki said, 'Whatever happened to the hybrid vigour that's meant to protect mongrels from ill health and evil conditions?'

So Cooper was on a literal short leash for ten days while his stitches were in. He was pretty good—didn't worry them and didn't require the 'cone of shame' to stop him licking at the wound—but it was hard for him to cope with just lead walks and no sticks and no games at home. 'What did I do wrong?' you could see him asking. Great was the joy the day the stitches, and then the Frisbee, came out.

COOPER WENT BACK FOR HIS second post-surgery check-up in early June, two months after the operation. This time, Sally found the lymph nodes at the front of his shoulder were enlarged. The area around the initial melanoma was fine and the lymph nodes under his front legs were okay, so it was a bit of a blow to hear Sally say the other ones were up. Bugger.

It could have been something completely different that had caused them to come up—a cut on his paw, for example, Sally posited—but I hadn't noticed anything. So she took small samples from both sides, sticking a needle into the front lymph nodes as best she could to see if there were melanoma cells there. If there were, god knows what we'd do. I didn't want to ask. But I knew enough to realise it would mean the cancer had spread already.

Sally was sort of confident it should be okay, but you never know how much of that is just jollying the worried owner. She kept saying how most melanomas she'd treated had a good outcome—but then, as I left, she noted that it was often the nice dogs like Cooper who had the worst outcomes. As I walked down the steps to the car, I wished she hadn't said that—that casual reflection deflating the little optimism she'd started to imbue me with.

As it turned out, there was nothing in the samples she'd taken that suggested the cancer had spread. So we waited, and watched, and held our breath some more. And everything seemed okay. But, in November, I took Cooper for his regular melanoma check and Sally noticed a wee lump near where the original one had been. She felt it and frowned, and shaved it and photographed it and sent the photos to an expert and said she'd ring me the next day after she heard from him—but her initial instinct was to remove it.

The expert had the same instinct when they saw the photos. Sally said if they were going to do surgery, she'd take out Cooper's prescapular lymph node—the one in front of his shoulder—while he was sedated to see if the cancer had actually spread, as those nodes were still slightly swollen. (Evidently, dogs don't need all their lymph nodes; they have several sets.)

I took Cooper in for surgery early the next morning.

I remembered what Sally had said after the first melanoma was removed: that, if the melanoma hadn't come back after six months, you could start to breathe more easily. This was seven months so, given I'd irrationally held her estimation to be a medical truth, it seemed bloody unfair it should have come back now.

I prepared myself for the worst. And, when Cooper came home with bandages and bald patches and stitches and painkillers and was woozy and whimpery, I just felt shit. And I couldn't help but wonder about the future. So I savoured every moment with him, and made promises to myself and to him that I would never be angry with him again. And I sort of wished I could make promises or deals with a god to make Cooper better, but I knew that was bullshittery and silliness—but you contemplate everything, for just a second.

A few days after the surgery, I had to go to Nelson, and I'd just got on the plane when my phone went. I could see it was the vet's number, but the cabin steward was earnestly doing her safety briefing, so I let it go and they left a message. As the steward finished up, and as the propeller outside my window picked up speed and we began taxiing, I quickly listened to the message. It was Pete, relaying the test results from the lump they'd cut off and the lymph nodes. The propellers began to drown out what he was saying, but I got the gist. All the tests were negative. Benign. I shut down my phone, turned towards the window and closed my eyes. I didn't want the passenger next to me to see the tears sliding down my face.

SOMETIMES NOW, I WATCH HIM licking that front paw and think, *Oh, shit. Can he feel something going on in his leg? Can his superior sensory intuition discern some irregular cell division going on?* And then I see him licking his left paw and reassure myself that it really is just preening.

And sometimes, I see him looking at me and it's like he's beseeching me to make sure he gets better. Your dog looks to you for everything, looks at you because they think you'll know the answers and you'll take care of them, no matter what happens. You're their security and comfort in so many ways. In reality, Cooper is probably just looking at me with his intense 'It's time to go for a walk' face, but I let myself think he's imploring, 'You'll make me better, won't you, Mike?'

I know he doesn't understand most of the words I say, but I still think I should whisper in his ear, 'I'll do everything I can.' That's not what he—or anyone, really —wants to hear, and it's not what I truly want to be able to tell him. But you can't lie, no matter how much you want it all to be otherwise. Some things are just beyond our control, and cancer is one of them.

And so, I see him looking at me and I feel nothing but guilt for not acting sooner, for offhandedly assuming that black nodule was just a knock-about scar. Why didn't I drive five minutes to have it checked out? The immediate response I retreat to is that I never knew dogs got melanoma—but that doesn't get me far in seeking any comfort, and nor does it seem in any way an answer Cooper would understand. Fuck.

POOR HARRY. ON A SUNNY winter morning at the dog park, he was feeling sprightly. He started chasing Cooper and Hamish and Aggie, and Barbro stood at the top of the hill, watching happily, and remarked, 'Oh, good, Harry is running.' There was a mix of pride that her eleven-year-old boy still had the will to sprint and relief that calories were being burned.

Down the hill they all raced, chasing a stick I'd flung into the long grass. Cooper bounded in to retrieve it, Hamish waited to bark at him, Aggie peeled off and began another circuit, and Harry scampered up behind her. But, as I watched, Harry suddenly stopped, looked around at his back leg and started limping. Of course, you hope he's just got something in his paw, but he continued carrying his leg as if it was injured. I went down to check him over but couldn't see anything, and Harry didn't seem overly perturbed besides not wanting to put any weight on the leg. Eventually, I offered to take him and Barbro home, and carried Harry back to the car, while he licked my face the whole way.

That evening, we got a dog park group email from Barbro: 'Harry forgot his age this morning and tore his posterior cruciate ligament, so will not be at the park for a while. Sob.' A week later, with little improvement, the vet recommended surgery. I'd feared as much; it's not the sort of thing that usually comes right with rest. Di's dog, Jess, had needed both her back legs operated on for the same problem. And the surgery isn't the worst part, it's the enforced inactivity afterwards as they heal: no walks, no playing, no jumping. Just excruciating immobility.

Harry recuperated from the operation patiently, while becoming a little more portly given his reduced exercise. I'd go around to see him, and receive the usual face-washing with gusto, while Katie yipped in the background. Then he'd lie on his back along the sofa, stretched out in all his glory, while I tickled him under his legs.

But partway through his recovery, Harry was upstairs and heard the front doorbell. He raced to investigate, tumbled down the stairs, aggravated his injury and was left limping again. Another trip to the vet resulted in Harry being given another month of sedentary life.

He eventually recovered well enough to return to the dog park and rejoin the gang of stick chasers, but there was something that never quite came right, his gait a fraction stifled. No matter. The dog park is not an arena for dressage contests.

ON A VISIT TO CENTRAL OTAGO in 2017, Nikki and I made a point of calling around to see artist Grahame

Sydney and his wife, Fi, who we'd got to know. They'd not long ago lost their three-legged ex-farm dog Gyp, and I knew their other dog, Milo, had been unwell and was losing his sight. I feared that, since I'd last had an update, Milo might have lost the battle. You know how it is—if you haven't heard anything for a while, you get too scared to ask how things are in case something awful has happened in the interim. But, thank goodness, Milo, now eleven, was still very much alive and it was so lovely to see him toddle in the door from outside. He was by now, however, completely blind, both eyes having had to be removed. Grahame and Fi had put a false eye on his right side to try to make him look more normal to other dogs. And they'd taped small white feathers around the sharp edges of furniture and kitchen benches and fireplace hearths so Milo would feel their touch before stumbling into anything.

He'd totter around quietly, knew where his water and food bowls were in the kitchen, and would happily cuddle into Grahame and Fi for long periods in front of the fire. At night, he'd curl up on an armchair at the foot of their bed with two blankets over him, and wouldn't stir till morning.

As Grahame said—and he felt this perhaps more keenly than most—he couldn't imagine losing the ability to see things. As an artist, that was how he lived. So to be robbed of it seemed almost as incomprehensible as it was horrifying. Perhaps the one comforting factor was that dogs rely so much more on their sense of smell to navigate the world than their sight.

The next morning, we saw Fi walking along a dry side road near St Bathans, and there was Milo, sniffing and marking the road's edge just like any other dog. From a distance, you'd never have guessed he couldn't see. Fi said they had to keep Milo on a lead during walks, otherwise he would race off and chase utes just as he always used to do. But, once home, he was free to roam. Why, just that morning, Fi said, Milo had spent an hour digging up a rabbit hole over the fence. Life was still a thrill, no matter how dark.

7.
The ways we
play with them

To walk into a pet shop is to enter a world that's bizarre and bemusing. To stare at its walls and displays and trudge its aisles is to realise how pet ownership has become a gigantic industry. A gigantic, lucrative and frequently idiotic one. The array of dog paraphernalia in particular should flummox anyone: there's a gizmo for every mood or occasion, expensive polycarbonate bowls, scientific leads, rectangles of faux grass so they can pee inside if it's cold. If all this isn't a sign we've gone mad, then it at least suggests we've gone way, way over the top.

But then I've been sucked in by it all in the past. When we picked up Cooper from the SPCA, I looked at the wall of leads and chews and balls and suchlike, and asked the woman if she'd recommend anything. She suggested a hard plastic ball about a third the size of a football, with a small opening in it. Through this hole, you placed tiny dog biscuits, then threw the ball out onto the lawn or wherever, and your dog had to learn to roll it around until the biscuits gradually came out of the hole. The SPCA woman said it would keep Cooper occupied for a bit and maybe stop him chewing the furniture out of boredom. So, in anxious preparation for bringing Cooper home, and with one eye on the survival of our modest furniture, we happily added it to the armful of other stuff we thought we needed.

And the ball was fine. After a few days of confusion, during which Cooper poked at it forlornly and we wondered if we'd adopted a simpleton, he finally got the hang of it. He would feverishly work away at it with his nose and paw on the back deck, rotating it till the hole was at the bottom and the biscuits began tumbling out. But it wasn't as if it gave him any real joy. It was always just a frustrating means to a meagre end; in his mind, an illogical impediment in his pursuit of food. As entertainment, it had neither attraction nor value in Cooper's view. I started wondering what else I should have spent that 30 bucks on.

The suspicion that the ball hadn't been a great investment was confirmed when Cooper dug out an empty plastic peanut-butter jar from the recycling bin and began playing with that instead. Man, he loved that jar. He'd chew on it and it would pop out of his mouth and skitter across the courtyard and he'd eventually corner it over by the garage and get his teeth into it, before jabbing at it with his paw and seeing it shoot off across the brickwork again so he could chase it. It provided endless hours of fun, while the specialised and costly doggy treats ball lay idle on the deck, like an abandoned fashion craze from last decade.

Right about then, I vowed never to buy Cooper another dog toy, because the world was already full of things—other things that he'd love equally or more.

But, of course, that commitment didn't last terribly long.

My previous dog, Cas, was fixated with one kind of toy: red practice cricket balls. They were the ideal size for her mouth, and just soft enough for her to get her teeth into yet were sufficiently weighted to fly for miles when thrown. I ordered them by the dozen from a company in Tauranga, and they were as precious to Cas as anything else in her world. Naively, I assumed Cooper would be equally besotted with them, and in premature excitement I bought a dozen from the Tauranga people. To say Cooper was disinterested is as fair and accurate as it was deflating for me. They may have been red and shiny and expensive, but he was far more interested in a worse-for-wear tennis ball dredged from a ditch or wrestled from under a gorse bush at the park.

It was an early lesson that every dog you own will be different. Just because you treat them and train them the same, just because the house and walks and biscuits and environs are the same, the likelihood is they'll all seem to come from different dog planets. There's no real surprise or science in that, but time and again you'll find yourself being reminded of it by your new dog, and like me, wondering what to do with twelve utterly untouched practice cricket balls.

WHILE CAS LIVED FOR HER red balls, she cowered from Frisbees. She'd sense this shape approaching in the sky, see a shadow swooping across the ground towards her and shrink in fright, like some small marsupial caught in the open as a raptor accelerates in for the kill. Cooper, however, never had any such qualms. And for this, and for his lifelong fascination with Frisbees, we have Bobby to thank. An Australian shepherd, Bobby was one of the first dogs Cooper met, and was certainly his idol for a long time. Bobby was named for the fact he had a bobtail— well, no tail, actually. It wasn't docked or deliberate, it's just how some of these puppies come out. Bobby was large and shaggy and a Frisbee grand master. He could read their flight, their angle, their trajectory and velocity. He could factor in Wellington winds and erratic throwers. He always perfectly predicted their arc and would be waiting for them. I watched and applauded. Cooper watched and learned.

Well, to be honest, at first Cooper couldn't have cared less about the finer points of a Frisbee's aerodynamics. He'd just wait for Bobby to catch it, then pounce and try to hustle him for it in an inelegant canine shakedown.

Bobby wasn't usually in the mood for that, and a tug-of-war would ensue, with other dogs swiftly joining in until it was a growling maul edging this way and that across the park. Sometimes, someone would lose their grip and the victor would circle us triumphantly. Often, the tussle would only be resolved by the tearing of fabric as the Frisbee ripped apart.

Bobby's owners were Doug and Carol. Doug was a skipper of the National Institute of Water and Atmospheric Research's scientific ship *Tangaroa*, and would often be away for weeks at a time, surveying distant seamounts or trenches. Carol worked in a costume shop and was a fabulous repository of dog knowledge. She watched dog-training programmes on TV, and would bring those lessons to the park with confidence and certitude. Where others fretted, Carol had answers and gave comfort to those with errant dogs.

It was to Carol that I usually had to apologise when I heard Bobby's Frisbee torn in two thanks to Cooper. And Carol was always great about it. 'No problem,' she'd say. 'I've got plenty. If you wait for them to be on special, they're only $10 from Kathmandu stores.' (Designed and marketed for children, I've only ever seen these Frisbees used by dogs, because they're soft yet fly really well.) So we'd wait till special day and grab a bunch to replenish Bobby's stock.

Gradually, Cooper learned that if he intercepted the

Frisbee in mid-air he could avoid the melee and tugs-of-war and prance away with the prize. He was good at catching things; it was just a matter of judging a Frisbee's fickle flight. Carol had told me that the TV programme *Dogs 101* had rated Australian shepherds like Bobby as the ultimate Frisbee dogs. I knew, therefore, that Cooper was training with the best. And after months of following Bobby with his calculated lope and sudden spring to snatch the Frisbee, Cooper got to be pretty good at it himself and remains an able exponent.

Bobby, though, was always the master, his devotion to the Frisbee unequalled. One time, when he had an injured leg, the Frisbees were confiscated and hidden under Doug's golf clubs at home while Bobby was supposed to be recuperating. Poor Bobby would make a beeline for anyone at the park who had one, ignoring Carol's shouts of 'Bobby, no!' and emoting with a frustrated whine when told he couldn't have it. Eventually, he found one of the Frisbees stashed under the golf clubs and appeared excitedly, dropping it at Carol and Doug's feet. They finally softened. Sometimes, the stress of denial is outweighed by the ease of normality.

We always keep a Frisbee in the back of the car, along with a stockpile of sticks and a ball-thrower. As Cooper bounds out for his walk, I test the wind and assess which is the most appropriate projectile. Given this is Wellington, most days it's not the Frisbee. I can't even guess how many

Kathmandu on-special Frisbees now rest decaying down an inaccessible gully or gently composting amid some impenetrable gorse thicket at the dog park. No matter how careful I think I'm being, an unforeseen gust will suddenly lift the Frisbee like a gull on a thermal, shift it at warp speed over any fence and take it out of sight forever. Whenever this happens, Cooper looks at me expectantly rather than accusingly, as if he thinks I can just conjure up another one. I look over the fence, assessing the likelihood of ever finding the Frisbee and thinking I might as well just be standing there throwing $10 notes with the wind.

Occasionally, it all ends in chaos. One day up at the park, my Frisbee flinging attracted the attention of another dog who raced up just as I threw it into a blasting northerly. It was a weak throw, easily matched by the wind, and the Frisbee flew straight back at me. Both Cooper and the new arrival were following the Frisbee, and all three of us went for it at the same time. I got there first, given my height advantage, but fumbled it and Cooper leaped for the rebound. In the mayhem and gale, my cap blew off, twirling like a sycamore pod, and was eagerly grabbed mid-air by the other dog, who naturally imagined it was a Frisbee of sorts. Both dogs danced a merry jig, parading their trophies. I just had to laugh, and hope the other dog gently reshaping my cap in its jaws understood the command 'drop'.

PROPERTY RIGHTS, OF COURSE, ARE a concept dogs struggle with. If there's a Frisbee at the park, their starting point is that it's probably theirs to claim. And that's fine, because most dog owners understand there's a certain amount of common possession at dog parks. But when non-dog owners arrive such equanimity is immediately stretched. One morning, I pulled up at Tanera dog park to see strange paint markings on the grass and wondered if this was the first step in some dastardly council plan to develop our space. But no, Mary Ellen informed me, it was the remains of an unfortunate afternoon where sharing the space became testy, then impractical.

Evidently, a group had decided the dog park would be the ideal place to stage an Ultimate Frisbee day, during which teams fling a disc among themselves down a field, in much the same way as American football or even soccer operates. Well, there were also about ten dogs there. And among them were Pug and Brook, sibling fox terriers who had been nourished on Frisbees ever since they were weaned and had minds of their own, as they say. Brook, in particular, was fearless. He once chased a seal near Wellington's Red Rocks, and when the seal slid into the water to escape, Brook launched himself from the rocks and landed on the seal's back as it swam away. The seal whipped around, grabbed Brook and held him under for at least ten seconds, before eventually releasing him. Brook made it back to shore, having sustained only deep puncture wounds around his shoulder.

Compared to wrestling seals, stealing Frisbees at the dog park was a cinch. And, following Pug and Brook's example, the remaining dogs also pretty quickly learned what fun it could be. It all ended predictably, with pissed-off Frisbee players demanding the dogs be restrained, dog owners suggesting they were idiots for planning their game at a dog park, and a bunch of dogs in high spirits thinking this was the best day ever. Realising it was hopeless, the Frisbee fraternity packed up and humphed off.

I missed that episode, alas, but I was there the glorious March morning a film crew decided to take over the park for a shoot. The dog walkers assessed them with interest, which soon became scepticism. The film crew eyed us as nuisances spoiling the emptiness of their location. They scoped the park with their cameras for optimum angles, looking suitably boho arty, as they held up their hands and peered through the frame their fingers formed.

Eventually, they came over to us and said could we please move, because we were in the way of their shot. So we ambled off towards the park bench on one side, and watched as they set up a scene with a young guy dressed in 1920s golfing attire preparing to drive a ball down the park. And that's when Louis, Matthew's massive Lab who would be a prop if he played rugby (Tony Woodcock, probably), spied that the action involved a ball. Louis is an opportunist, especially if there's discarded food around.

But if there's no food, then a ball is the next best thing. So Louis lumbered over and gobbed the golf ball before the actor could swing his club, then happily pranced away looking extraordinarily pleased with himself, rolling the ball around his mouth and double-coating it in drool. Eventually, Matthew retrieved the ball from him and the actors started setting up again.

This time, the action involved another actor, angrily yelling something about the queen and 'You'll be sleeping with the rats'. Well, this was unusual and unsettling behaviour at the dog park, or so thought Bonnie, who immediately raced towards the shouty man and stood about five metres away, growling. Then the fluffy poodly pair, Stan and Ernie, sensed danger and joined in, roaring up and barking. The shouty actor, by this stage, was half bent forward, nervously proffering his hand towards the three growly outriders and going, 'Good dogs. Nice dogs. Come here.' Both film crew and dog walkers were in fits of laughter.

Jeremy then thought he'd add further dog action to the visitors' art, and started lobbing tennis balls towards them, arcing them over the set with a ball-thrower so his dog, Lola, ran through the shot. Sensing something exciting was going on, other dogs began barking, adding an unwanted soundscape for the film crew.

We could see we weren't helping or wanted, so decided to decamp for work, chuckling a bit as we called our dogs and made our way up the path. Ceri reckoned the location scout would have been fired by morning-tea time. But you had to have a bit of sympathy for them, given they'd come across this wonderful grassy park with views over the harbour and city . . . and a whole lot of dogs each morning who really like chasing balls.

The guy who used to practise his gymnastics at the park was another who undoubtedly thought he'd discovered a perfect place to train, without giving sufficient thought to the location. A stunning outlook over Wellington? Yep. Sturdy trees to loop his equipment over so he could hang from the rings like Olympians do? Yep. Dogs that thought this was pretty curious and really interesting? Yep, that too. I have a clear memory of this free spirit dangling from the pōhutukawa, upside down in something of an inverted crucifix, with a dog sniffing his face. It might have been Cooper. It's been a long time since the gymnast dangled at the dog park.

BALLS, OF COURSE, ARE THE go-to toy for any dog— particularly tennis balls, and our park has some of the finest examples on offer. This is largely due to its proximity to Wellington's premier courts at the Renouf Tennis Centre. Tennis is all about exertion and action, but this doesn't seem to apply when a ball flies over the fence and into the surrounding scrub. Walk around the edge of any tennis court and you'll find proof of this perplexing truth.

Matthew will often take Louis on a loop of the Renouf Centre and arrive at the dog park with a bag full of at least 20 balls, which he'll distribute among those gathered. The best thing is, these aren't the cheap crap tennis balls you get at pet shops or hardware stores, which split at first chomp or slip their furry skins as soon as they get damp. No, these are top-of-the-line pro balls—Slazenger, Dunlop, Prince—that last and bounce nearly forever. The only, and obvious, problem is that they're shades of green, and so is the majority of the dog park. (Right here, I'll mention there's a sociological split between those who say tennis balls are green and those who insist they're yellow. I'm in the green camp.) So, if the grass is a little long, finding them can be tricky. Often you give up, and their location is only revealed weeks later when the council comes by to mow the park and leaves a trail of scalped tennis balls in their wake, forsaken rubber demitasses.

But the realm of tennis balls and dogs has been forever changed and augmented since the development of the ball-thrower. Whoever invented it, whoever imagined the potential of a gentle curve of extruded plastic, whoever foresaw the possibilities of updating the catapult for the benefit of pet owners was a genuine mastermind who deserves to be really rich. Essentially, ball-throwers have a handle at one end, a cup that perfectly fits a tennis ball at the other, and they're connected by a length of bent plastic up to 60 centimetres long. This allows you to pick up a tennis ball without bending down or touching the horrible slobbery thing and launch it far further than any normal throw, due to the flex and flick of the thrower as you whip it forward.

It's simplicity, but genius. It's a saver of shoulder joints and bicep muscles. It's a few bucks of fundamental dog kit everyone should have at hand, or at least stashed somewhere in their car.

But the king of dog toys, in my mind and certainly in Cooper's, remains the stick. The humble, ubiquitous, eternally varied stick. Dogs and sticks go together like, oh, I don't know, chips and aioli, or cats and toxoplasmosis: they perhaps shouldn't, but you can't get away from them. Clever people have suggested that a dog's fixation with sticks has to do with replicating prey or bones, although that seems a stretch to me. They opine that stick chewing is part of a dog's 'oral fixation' and it helps clean their gums and teeth, as if they've been swept up in some dental health movement. I think it's just natural, something almost genetic, something born of necessity before a world of pet products arrived and provided alternatives. Sticks are plentiful, they fly, they float, there are sizes for all. They seem quite perfect for dogs.

If a single imagined scene could sum up the joy of owning a dog for me, it would be a sketch of a boy and a dog, a stick soaring high and weightless between them. To me, that would encapsulate the sheer pleasure of walking

a dog—the outdoors, the exercise, the play, the chase, the companionship, the shared fun. Just distilled delight for both boy and dog, and one I've fortunately experienced. But, to an increasing lobby group, such a scene would be pure irresponsibility and indescribable danger. Because sticks have become enemies, arboreal evils, cited by vets as the cause of frequent injury as they splinter and wound dogs. At worst, they jam down their throats and cause death.

I read a story in *The Guardian* a couple of years ago which contained the direst of warnings from the British Veterinary Association about sticks. The spokesperson mentioned occasions when dogs had been impaled, when spinal cords had been pierced, when blood vessels had been punctured causing fatal blood loss. 'One dog had developed holes in its head after part of a stick had become trapped across its back molars and had eroded its hard palate,' the story quoted a vet saying. Holes in the dog's head? It seemed it wasn't a tragic one-off. A dog behaviourist called Stan Rawlinson claimed he'd seen 'one dog who caught a stick that, spear-like, went straight through its head'. Jeez. You start having horror visions. But you also start wondering what kind of stick was thrown for the dog. A javelin?

'Sticks are dangerous,' Rawlinson decreed, and that was that.

But then, when reader reaction was unleashed in the story's comments section, even more hidden horrors at playtime were revealed. One person noted that a 'tennis ball can become lodged in the dog's throat, causing difficulty in breathing. I have always bought a ball that has a hole in it for this reason'. To which someone responded, 'A basketball is safer . . .'

Of course, there were plenty of people who railed against the over-the-top protectionism the story encouraged— 'How dangling a bit of string for your cat could lead to accidental garroting'—and linked it to *The Guardian*'s liberal line. 'How incredibly, staggeringly Guardianista can you get? Next week: how kissing your grandmother damages the ozone layer.' And that caused someone to aim directly at the heart of *Guardian* parishioners used to environmental high priest George Monbiot's climate change columns. 'Tomorrow, Monbiot will be here to tell us that the sudden spike in demand for oil-derived dog toys is destroying our world even quicker than before.'

Someone suggested throwing dogs a rolled-up *Guardian* instead. Someone else then suggested throwing sticks at *Guardian* journalists. 'They would consider it appropriation of canine culture and write a po-faced article about it,' another replied.

But the thing that struck me as I scrolled through the responses was how witty and eloquent most commenters were. It seemed a different world to New Zealand news websites, where after about three thoughtful comments intelligent debate is usually abandoned and commenters start attacking each other like dogs at each other's throats. 'Fuck you.' 'No, fuck you.' 'Stupid arsehole.' 'Moron.' 'Nazi.' Here, the debate ranged from free will to Darwinism to evidence-based dog play, to concern at statistical accuracy: 'According to White & Lane (1988) the throat is "one of the least frequently traumatised sites of the head and neck".'

When someone suggested 'Just throw a ball', the swift response from another reader was: 'Tried that once. Turns out dogs are shit at dancing, but a right handful when they've been at the punch.'

But perhaps the comment that got to the heart of the story's validity and veracity—at least from a dog's perspective—was: 'No. Throw it again. No. Throw it again. No. Throw it again.'

That one got lots of likes. I was tempted to add one.

Because that's exactly and inarguably what goes through Cooper's head and comes out of his mouth in the form of incessant barking each morning at the park. (Though I recently saw a great cartoon with a guy about to throw a stick and his dog going, 'OK, just one more, and then I've got to get on with my life.') For Cooper, no other toy or entertainment will do—just the biggest stick possible, hiffed into the bushes, where he plays games of his own invention, getting his nose underneath the stick, flicking it in the air and catching it. It's sort of feral rhythmic gymnastics.

I don't know how his stick fixation started. I'd like to think it wasn't my fault, as we provided him with other options to chase in the form of balls and Frisbees, which he will play with elsewhere. But Tanera Park is a stick-only zone for him.

When he was younger, Cooper would happily share his stick with Harry and Mackenzie, the three of them sometimes latching on to it and moving around in slow union like yoked animals, only to finally collapse together and chew on it. Since then, Cooper has grown up and seemingly grown out of sharing his sticks. Other dogs attempting a heist of his stick get a growling.

Inevitably, there have been minor accidents. I have clunked him on the head a couple of times as I misjudged my throw, or he was faster to arrive than the stick. And there was the time our friend Jan was walking him, threw a stick and heard him yelp, then Cooper started drooling and looking miserable in the car on the way home. We sped him to the vet, who manoeuvred his mouth to see if a shard was lodged down there, but couldn't see anything other than a possible abrasion where a stick might have caught him. She gave him pain relief and gave me an eyeballing. She was restrained, but I clearly knew I was being reprimanded for throwing sticks and thus endangering my dog. I slunk out of the vet clinic and watched Cooper intently all night for signs of deterioration, but there were no after-effects.

The next day, admonished and determined to change my ways, I grabbed the pseudo stick I had at home as we headed off for our walk. Let me tell you about these things. They're called Kong Safestix, are made from some kind of rubber–silicone composite and come in small, medium or large sizes. They are flexible, ribbed like rope and have bulbous ends. Without dancing around in further descriptions, they essentially and unfortunately look like a sex toy.

Angsting about possible stick injuries for Cooper, we had ordered a couple of Safestix online some months earlier. While you can choose the size—we opted for the 50-centimetre medium version—you aren't able to specify colour. So what turned up in the post was a day-glo pink one and a luminous lime green one. Now, it's a long way from an earthy and rugged stick to a two-foot lipstick-pink sex-toy lookalike, but Cooper, bless him, made that journey with little protest. But only at home. Because that's where we kept the Kong (which somehow, by someone, got renamed the schlong). Because, for seemliness, that's where it belonged. Because, when a young courier driver one day spied me throwing it to Cooper by the gate, he couldn't believe what he was seeing and pleaded to have a closer look at the thing. Next minute, he was in the cab of his van taking selfies holding the schlong around his crotch to send to his mate.

So, for exactly this reason, I'd never taken the Kong

schlong to the dog park, or to any other public space. But, following the stick incident and the vet's rebuke, I decided I should put Cooper's safety before my concerns about propriety and what people might say, and threw the pink one in the car as we set off for the dog park that morning. I made sure I arrived early, before the rest of the dog-walking regulars, and in a gap between the commuters who stride to the city through the park. Cooper raced down the path to the first grassy flat as usual to await me hurling a stick. I lobbed the pink thing towards him and it landed nearby, garishly out of place in a world of green and brown. Cooper barely flinched. He half-glanced at this thing lying beside him, then reverted to staring at me. This wasn't the routine. This wasn't what we played at the park. This certainly was no stick.

I looked around to make sure nobody was watching us, and I flung it again, exhorting Cooper to chase it. He remained rooted to the spot, gaze still fixed on me, sure that I'd produce the real stick after this bit of nonsense. I again checked for onlookers and, seeing nobody, picked up the pink thing and lobbed it from close range at Cooper for him to catch. It hit him in the face, and he looked both worried and wounded by this indignity. I waggled it in front of his face and he looked perplexed. Had I forgotten what the game was? It was a park. It was full of sticks. 'Just go and get one, Mike.'

A man walked by, and I moved several steps from the

rejected pink thing and pretended not to have noticed it. As soon as he'd passed, I made a break for it, swooped on the pink thing, thrust it under my jacket, jogged up the path back to the car and threw it inside. I grabbed a real stick, and headed back to Cooper.

WHEN YOU WALK A DOG and throw sticks for them, your view of the world changes. Everything from a broken branch to an outsized twig becomes a potential dog toy. You pass a stick on the path and pause, instantly weighing its mass and merit, and whether it's worth putting in the car for Cooper's future use. You measure its length, its weight, its resilience; assess the crook and likely aerodynamics. Too light and it won't fly far. Too heavy and you'll scone your dog or wrench your wrist. Ideally, it should be smooth so it won't rip your hand as you release it or chafe your dog's mouth when he retrieves it. It should be a bit thinner than, say, a broom handle at one end and bit fatter at the other, so as to give it optimal heft. A slight curve is fine. Around a metre long is good. Any stubs from side branches should be burred flat. It should be free of cracks or splintering skin.

I often collect sticks from the beach that are desiccated by the sun, their surfaces worn smooth by waves and sand. They're almost ideal, though prone to shattering. The dog park, surrounded by trees, offers a vast range of options, but usually all with imperfections.

One morning I arrived at the park to find the remains of a party someone had held the previous afternoon. There were fragments of burst pink balloon, some trampled flowers, a squashed spring onion and a very nice wine glass wedged between the pōhutukawa's branches. And underneath the tree was an abandoned croquet mallet. Once Cooper saw me holding it, he dropped the stick we'd been playing with and waited, front paw cocked, ready for me to throw this wondrous new thing. To him, it wasn't a sporting tool; it was the most fantastic, shiny stick he'd ever seen. And it was magnificent, but its heavy hammerhead made it difficult to throw and nearly impossible for Cooper to balance in his mouth. After a couple of tries, we replaced it under the pōhutukawa and returned to our less glamorous, unvarnished model.

A perfect stick is a hard thing to find.

And so, when I do find something worthy, I try to keep it. I've brought sticks back from Kāpiti Coast beaches and from the bush of the Tararuas because they were rare perfection. Barbro, pandering to my obsession, once returned from Motueka with a selection of sticks for Cooper to choose from.

However, the value of a good stick is lost on those whose dogs find fascination in balls, or prefer to just stand and contemplate. When a near-flawless stick I'd had for weeks split at one end, I bound it with insulating tape so it wouldn't injure Cooper and kept hurling it. Others at the park looked mystified and presumed the tape was to make it easier on my palms. I didn't bother explaining too much, knowing how daft it would all sound. Only fellow stick adherents would appreciate that not all sticks are equal.

The best sticks are returned to the car, unless some other mutt has nicked it from Cooper and made off with it or chewed its end to a ragged stump. Sometimes I'll stash sticks in trees at the park—emergency backups in case I lose the original choice from the car. And, man, I lose a lot. Despite years of stick-hurling practice, I'm adept only at hooking my throw or wafting the stick too high, so it sits jammed and marooned in the upper branches of some leafy sapling at the park's edge. When this happens, I make good and determined efforts to free the stick, sometimes climbing the tree, but more often standing at its base, grabbing the appropriate branch and shaking madly till it tumbles free.

Passers-by must wonder what lunatic inhabits the shrubbery at Tanera Park when they notice a tree beside the path quivering violently on a calm day and a voice from the deep green depths mumbling, 'Come down, you bastard . . .'

WE FAREWELLED MARY ELLEN WITH odd abruptness. She'd been one of the very first people I'd met at the park with her cairn terrier, Mackenzie, who looked like a slightly fluffy wombat. Originally from the States, she'd been in New Zealand a while, and spent several years living near Lake Ohau—hence Mackenzie's name—before her allergies forced her to relocate to Wellington and its salty air.

In those early days, there would frequently be just Barbro and Mary Ellen and me at the park of a morning. Me feeling ignorant, as they considered the world and debated whether Roman Polanski should be sent back to America to stand trial for rape, the value of utilitarianism, and a diverse daily panoply of weighty issues. I'd listen, contribute little, then sidle off to fling a stick for Cooper.

Mary Ellen had received a call from her brother in America concerned about her parents' well-being and their need to shift into supported living. On Wednesday Mary Ellen handed in her notice at the Productivity Commission, and by Friday had cleared her desk. By the following Wednesday she and Mackenzie were on a plane to San Francisco. The intervening days were filled with all manner of preparations, but none that occupied Mary Ellen as much as arranging Mackenzie's transport and comfort. This included accusatory and angry correspondence with Air New Zealand about the conditions Mackenzie would have to endure on the flight across the Pacific. She wanted Mackenzie with her in the cabin—an unlikely and reasonably unrealistic request. But Mary Ellen saw things differently. She argued that if it was good enough for a bloody kākāpō to have a box and its own seat on Air New Zealand flights, then what was the difference if it was a dog? She argued that, once in the States, Mackenzie could travel with her as cabin baggage in first class, so why couldn't she do that here? She argued she was prepared to pay for the seat.

Air New Zealand remained unmoved, though Mary Ellen's request did go right to the top. Somehow, she had managed to get hold of the private email of Air New Zealand's CEO at the time, Rob Fyfe, and even though he was laid up in hospital after minor surgery he personally replied to her. The upshot was that, although Mackenzie wasn't allowed in the cabin, she was met in Auckland by her own dedicated Air New Zealand staff member, who took her to a special transit room then personally stood by the plane and oversaw her loading. Once she got to San Francisco, Mackenzie was met by special ground staff and given treatment akin to returning Olympic gold medallists or foreign royalty, before boarding her flight to Minnesota in first class, in a small carrier under Mary Ellen's feet.

So we had a final morning with Mary Ellen at the park on the day she left, sitting on the grass, sitting in the sun. Mary Ellen produced a bag of leftover dog treats and superfluous toys for us to choose from. Cooper inherited a miniature tractor tyre attached to a purple rope, with which to play tug-of-war and likely wrench my shoulder from its floppy socket.

I was amazed Mackenzie had so many toys, because she'd never exhibited any eagerness to play at the park since I'd been there. Maybe she was just getting older. When they lived at Lake Ohau, Mackenzie evidently would grab shoes and take off with them, particularly gumboots. So Mary Ellen had bought her a pair of kids' Red Bands, forced to admit to the woman in the shop who asked about sizing that they were for her dog.

Mackenzie's gumboots were already packed away for the relocation, and the remaining toys held little interest for her that morning. Instead, she lay beside Harry, her best dog friend, the two of them chewing opposite ends of the same stick—the canine equivalent of a long, lingering hug.

8.
The ways they shame us

The very first thing Cooper did, when we brought him home for the very first time, was something disreputable. In the gate he went, still on his new lead, towing us behind him, making a beeline for some fresh cat shit the neighbour's tabby hadn't bothered to bury. The SPCA woman's words were still warm in my ears from minutes before: 'Your life won't be the same again,' she'd sung out, as we headed for the car with our new pup. While I attempted to extract cat shit from Cooper's mouth and stuff it back under the neighbour's fence, I tried to imagine this wasn't quite what she had in mind. It certainly wasn't what I had in mind when I had looped my signature on the adoption papers.

No matter how proud you are of your dog, no matter how good your dog is, they'll shame you at some point. Quite a few points, generally. More often than not, it's to do with eating, and the things they'll chew and rip and swallow, which range from sheer filth to the quite inexplicable. After the cat-shit incident, we got off pretty lightly with Cooper. He wasn't a terrible chewer, apart from the odd soft toy that got disembowelled, fluffy guts scattered throughout the bedroom and lounge. Our furniture, such as it was, survived puppyhood unscathed.

There was the time, however, when Nikki put some coffee grounds around the newly planted broccoli seedlings to ward off snails, and curious Cooper decided they were for him. Not long after, he was running around the house with a plastic pot stuck on his head. Wired was certainly one way to describe him, as he pranced to and fro like a lunatic, uprooted broccoli in his wake.

But the worst incident was the time I returned home to find several books lying dismembered across the floor of my office—all torn pages, shredded covers and reconfigured photos. Of course, at times like this, it's never the books you couldn't care less about that get destroyed, the ones you've only kept out of obligation or superstition. And in this case, it was even worse: the targets weren't even mine, they were library books, borrowed to research a story I was writing.

So, there lay *They Gave Us Rugby*, by Alan Turley, with foreword by Keith Quinn, and *Rugby: The Pioneer Years*, also by the industrious Alan Turley. Pages 131 to 146 of the former were mutilated on the diagonal, and by the time I rescued it the picture of the first-ever New Zealand team, which toured Australia in 1884, was missing the back and most of the centre rows. The books' covers were either gone or riddled with tooth marks, like a rural road sign some drunk bogan has peppered with a shotgun. The jacket of Michael King's *The Penguin History of New Zealand*, which had been plucked off the bookshelf when Cooper got bored with rugby, had simply been flensed, with no consideration for the book's near-biblical status in New Zealand's cultural canon.

I stood there, bag in one hand, keys in the other, and scanned the literary flotsam. Cooper sat in the middle of it all, scanning my face for indications of anger and eyeing a possible escape route in case things went bad. But what do you do? You can't ask him to explain himself, let alone demand he Sellotape up the damage.

Any explaining was my responsibility, so, the next day, I slunk into the library, buggered books in hand and a pathetic excuse on my lips. I mean, telling a librarian your dog ripped up their books seems as credible as telling your college teacher the same thing happened to your homework. Implausibility coated every word of my excuse, but, remarkably, the librarian cheerily accepted it. Said it happened all the time. Charged me $25 and smiled as she handed me the receipt. Even though I knew it was the truth, I felt like I'd just got away with a petty criminality. I'm guessing Cooper felt much the same.

HOBBS, MEANWHILE, WAS A RIGHT bugger when it came to eating things. Well, not many things, but, curiously, his leads. Nikki picked up Cooper and Hobbs one day and saw Cooper's new lead had been mysteriously severed. She stitched it up and discovered it was shorter than it had been previously, but figured the remainder might have been lost in the garden when the boys were playing tug-of-war or somesuch.

Later that week, I popped Cooper and Hobbs in the car and stopped at the supermarket on our way for a walk. When I let them out at the park, Cooper's lead was only about 30 centimetres long—the handle had completely disappeared, and what was left dangling from his neck was sodden with slobber. I hunted for the missing bit but couldn't find anything in the car, and naively assumed Hobbs had chewed through Cooper's lead and the rest must have somehow fallen out.

But, four days later, the truth emerged when Hobbs puked up half a metre of red lead. The same thing happened several times after that.

You can't begin to fathom it really. It's not delicious, it's not food and it sure wouldn't be easy to swallow. But, to this day, if you leave Hobbs's lead on him when he's in the back of the car, he'll have a crack at it.

It's not as if Hobbs isn't well fed, or is perpetually hungry. When he was young, he didn't really care about food—apart from Cheezels, which he found irresistible.

For a while, during a brief spell as a delinquent youth, Hobbs wouldn't come to you when he was having too much fun playing at the park. So we would all have an emergency bag of Cheezels stashed in the car glove box in order to lure him close enough to grab.

At night when they went to bed, his owners, Jan and Briar, would leave a Tux biscuit on his beanbag as a goodnight treat. The following morning, for several months, when they got up they'd find a bunch of books had fallen from the bookcase and were lying on the floor. Their cats usually got the blame. Eventually, Briar discovered the true cause—and a pile of uneaten Tux biscuits that Hobbs had been stashing at the back of the bookcase. Like I say, you could spend ages trying to rationalise this kind of stuff.

Tales of dogs scoffing a box of chocolates and having their stomach pumped (chocolate is generally considered poisonous for dogs) aren't uncommon. Kirsty got a $450 vet bill from one of Barney's Yuletide raids. And the bill mounted well past that for Gin, whose hairy monster of a dog, Jake, had a shoe fetish. He ransacked her wardrobe and reconfigured a number of work shoes when he was a pup, but when Jake took a fancy to the pair Gin had got in New York the year before, it caused tears. And, of course, it's never both shoes that they chew to bits—so you always end up throwing away one pristine, beautiful, but useless Jimmy Choo or whatever, which seems to double the tragedy.

You turn your back for half a minute with dogs, and savagery will have occurred. When Jeremy's partner, Carlena, was heading overseas one time, she laid out everything she was taking on the bed, in an impressive spread of preparedness. Then she left the room. By the time she returned, Lola was happily chowing down on her passport. Thank goodness for that emergency replacement service.

But without doubt, the most inglorious thing dogs ingest is the shit of other dogs. It's the habit that dares not speak its name, although it does have a name: coprophagia. It's something puppies often do, and there are a bunch of explanations for why, including balancing their microbiome and getting nutrients they may be missing in their diet. All the science and justification in the world won't matter a jot, however, when it's your dog who does it. All you want to do is get them home quickly and give them the domestic version of waterboarding by sluicing their face with a high-pressure hose, then insist they don't come anywhere near you for the rest of the day.

Bonnie is the sweetest of dogs, a silken-haired something who leans into your shins for a tickle and daintily raises a front leg so you can better reach her belly. She wears a rainbow-coloured collar that makes you want to sing 'We Are the World'. But she has a weakness for wolfing down other dogs' poo, and her owner, Diana, is left mortified. 'It's disgusting,' she whispers.

'It's an eating disorder,' I say, trying to be helpful.

Of course, you don't broadcast such galling behaviour, and it's only shared with trusted dog park confidantes. Sometimes, though, the secret slips out, the vile habit incontrovertibly exposed. Once, when she was going away on holiday, Diana dropped Bonnie off to a friend who lived around Wellington Harbour. They did the handover at Petone Beach, and during the transfer Bonnie ran around and sniffed and snuffled and then went home with Diana's friend. When Diana picked up Bonnie at the end of the weekend, the friend said she'd been a delight and could come back any time. Diana double-checked and said, 'Are you sure there were no problems?' And the friend said, 'Oh, well, only one . . .' It seemed that, when Bonnie had got home from Petone Beach, she had barfed up on the rug. Which was bad enough, but what she barfed up was another dog's turd that she'd scarfed up along the beach.

As hard as it is, just keep that image in your mind next time you're thinking about getting a puppy, cooing at those oh-so-cute photos, won over by the prospect of love and licks and imagining it's all going to be fluff and joy.

THE LIST OF DISGRACEFUL DOG habits is extensive, the shadow of shame they cast over you a long one. Ask any dog owner and they will be able to come up with examples of infamy specific to their dog, but a few are universal.

Humping strangers' legs is among the most disreputable. Simulated sex is just one of those things you can't make light of or pretend was an innocent mistake. And chopping their bits off doesn't cure such flagrancy. Ziggy the vizsla used to be a notorious humper and his owner, Clare, couldn't wait for the appointment with the vet to have his nuts removed. But, after the operation, Ziggy would just stand at the dog park and hump nothingness, grinding away into the air by himself. Clare was aghast and wanted her money back. We reasoned it was probably just residual testosterone or hormones or whatever still stuck in his system, and whatever it was would eventually work its way out and he'd calm down.

Ceri's dog, Leo, is the loveliest animal, a velvety black labradoodle who is a friend to all new arrivals at the park, and a hopeful lover of many. When Leo is in the mood for love, Ceri has to follow him around, interceding and hauling him off as he makes friends from behind, in front of or at the side of other dogs. I tell her Leo is just playing, and it's a wrestling hold. But she knows I don't really believe what I'm saying—she knows a blatant mounting manoeuvre when she sees one. And claiming clemency on the basis of true love will only ever get you so far.

Dogs roll in evil stuff and are experts at getting it all around their collar, where it's really hard to wash off and will reek for days. They'll rip open your garbage bag or your neighbour's one. They'll bark at birds, passing dogs, skateboarders, meter readers and mere phantoms of their imagination. They certainly bark at the postie—well, Cooper definitely does.

And dogs dig. They'll uproot your pot plants, leaving gasping seedlings strewn across your paths, and vandalise your precious vegetable patch. They never dig out weeds— have you noticed that? Just the valuable and vital and beloved stuff. Cooper, fortunately, has never been a huge digger, except when he's at the beach and sand will fly in all directions till he's created a small meteorite crater. The odd bone gets buried at home, but that's usually a half-hearted effort that involves shovelling a lot of dirt over it with his nose.

However, for a while, he was constantly digging a hole under our karo tree behind the garage. I'd come out to find dirt sprayed over the courtyard and get grumpy, but there was no point in growling at him because I never caught him in the act. Then, one day, I went outside to find another fresh pile of dug dirt, and on top of it was a small plastic toy animal. It looked like a German shepherd— brown, shaggy, long-legged. It could have been a wolf in winter coat, I guess, but I preferred to think it was a dog. So I brought it inside, and now the plastic ancestor that Cooper discovered sits on the windowsill above his bed. And he's never dug in that spot since.

THEN THERE ARE CATS. I HAVE absolutely no idea what it is about cats that sets Cooper off. He is uninterested and unmoved by every other creature, but put him anywhere near a cat and he's transformed into a would-be killer with a startling turn of speed down the pavement. There's just something about them that bucks reason and defies discipline.

A couple of times a year, we housesit for our friends Deborah and Colin, who have a small vineyard near Martinborough. They also have a small safari park of animals from pigs to horses to ducks to chooks. We stayed there a few days after we first got Cooper, and figured it would be the perfect place to teach him to leave other animals alone. And it's worked, mostly.

He ignores the resident dogs with embarrassing haughtiness. He barely casts a glance at the sheep in the neighbouring paddock. He is bemused by the grunting pigs. He allows rabbits to share the lawn without fear of violence. He cedes right of way to the chooks and bantams as they strut and shit where it suits. But he is death to the cats, a right prick who will launch himself off the veranda in frantic pursuit of them if they dare stray around his side of the house. I have simply no idea why, and swear it's not taught behaviour; it's just utterly instinctual, possibly genetic, it seems.

Maybe it all goes back to that first time we were at Deborah and Colin's and I tried to engineer some cross-species bonhomie between Cooper and one of the cats, Kete. It was all looking promising, with each gingerly nosing the other while I made stupid cooing noises beside them and wittered on about everyone being friends. Then, in a blink, Kete lashed out with her paw. She missed Cooper, but her claws neatly sliced open the palm of my hand. Kete calmly and wisely retreated to an unreachable sanctuary under a chair. Cooper looked perplexed. I bled everywhere.

There is no way this could have sparked Cooper's incorrigible habit of chasing cats. But whenever he does give Kete a run for her money across the vineyard, I'm tempted to argue that she started it.

CATS DID IT FOR OTTO, too, but were almost his downfall. Otto was owned by Clare and Nick, who live in the property adjoining the bottom of the dog park. A Jack Russell, Otto was feisty as hell and a dab hand at absconding. The good thing about this was that, after Clare and Nick got him, they got to meet a whole lot more people—neighbours, construction site managers, random strangers—who all discovered Otto when he escaped, looked at the tag on his collar and rang Clare. 'I think I've got your dog . . .' The downside was that eternal vigilance was required to stop him going AWOL and possibly being run over by a car while roaming.

One time, as the family was packing to leave for a holiday, one of the kids left the gate open, and Otto sniffed freedom and fled. Out into the park, down the path beside the community gardens, across Ohiro Road, Clare and the kids in fairly frantic pursuit. Once on the other side of the road, Otto spied a cat and gave chase. Threading through traffic, the pair crossed back over the road, skidded down a driveway and barrelled head first through a cat flap and into a house. By the time Clare and the kids panted their way to the front door of the stranger's house, all they could hear was Otto barking his head off somewhere inside.

Peering through the cat flap, they could just see him, head cocked upwards, staring at his quarry, as if the cat was up on a shelf or bookcase. They tried calling him, but he was much too busy barking. They tried to find an open window or door, but everything was locked. They rifled through the mail in the letterbox to try to get a name and find a phone number, but with no luck.

One of the kids then ran home to get some sausages, which they broke into pieces and began tossing through the cat flap in an attempt to entice Otto back outside. No chance. Otto enjoyed sausage as much as any dog, but the opportunity to corner a cat was a rare event and at that moment it was taking all his attention.

By now, Clare was at breaking point and devising ways of breaking into the house to get Otto. Exasperated, she rang Nick and told him she was sick of dealing with

Otto and he could come and sort it out. But then one of the kids, who had remained resourceful while their parents were dreaming of a) becoming petty burglars or b) murdering Otto when they got him out, snapped a couple of toetoe stalks off a bush in the garden and lashed them together. A piece of sausage was jammed onto the end of the makeshift spear and it was then inserted through the cat flap. Crouching and peering and cajoling, they managed to get it just close enough to Otto's nose that he couldn't resist the sausage. At which point, they retracted the spear and Otto was lured back towards the door and eventually came close enough that they could grab him by the neck through the cat flap and haul him out.

What would have happened if the homeowners had returned a few minutes before this and found a strange family desperately huddled around their front door with a bag of sausages and a dog going nuts inside is a scene so delightful to imagine it's worth lingering on. But the reality was more prosaic. The residents, whoever they were, would have got home to find their toetoe looking slightly the worse for wear, and their kitchen scattered with sausage. The cat, doubtless still traumatised and possibly still on top of the bookcase, would have then got the bollocking of its life for stealing somebody's sausages, dragging them home and leaving them throughout the house.

THE COMEDY OF OTTO, THE cat and the sausages had a sad coda, however. Not long afterwards, Otto and the family went to Waikanae for a weekend. While there, Otto escaped once too often; his luck ran out and he was hit and killed by a car. He was buried at home.

OHIRO ROAD, WHICH ESSENTIALLY demarcates one edge of Tanera dog park, is a busy and treacherous thorough-fare. It's narrow, twisting and used by cars and cyclists as a shortcut between Aro Valley and Brooklyn. It's not a place for dogs to stray. So, when a large German shepherd who was muzzled but still managing to be aggressive bowled Bonnie over at the park one weekend, she was spooked enough to run for home. Home was about 500 metres up Ohiro Road. By the time Diana and her three kids realised Bonnie had scarpered, she was out of sight. Search parties were dispatched in various directions and Diana rushed home with her younger son, Bruno, panicking that Bonnie would be run over and found dying in a gutter somewhere on Ohiro Road.

Bruno, jogging alongside her, was more sanguine than sad at this prospect. 'It's okay. We'll just get another one,' he said, with a shrug. 'Or a cat,' he added, with some enthusiasm.

By the time they reached their front door, Bonnie was waiting for them, having somehow negotiated three ghastly intersections to make her way home. Bonnie got a hug. Bruno didn't get a cat.

OF COURSE, SOMETIMES IT'S NOT the dogs who get bowled over. Sometimes, it's the attendant humans who get flattened by dogs. I know a bit about this, given dogs have broken a couple of my bones. When I was four, I got skittled by our dog at the time, Sandy the cocker spaniel. Sandy wasn't the fastest thing on four legs—not what you'd consider an athletic dog. But, every now and then, he'd go crazy and sprint around as if seized by the ghost of a greyhound. On one of these rare occasions, I unfortunately happened to be rounding the corner of our house at the same moment Sandy came flying the other way. A broken collarbone resulted.

And then, when I was a teenager, I was running down the pavement with Gyp on my left only for him to spy a cat to my right, skulking under a bush on my mate Tim Wilson's front lawn. Bloody cats. Gyp instantly changed course 90 degrees to chase the cat, cut straight in front of me and left me spreadeagled on the pavement. That one broke my wrist.

So, when I met Peter Bush at Tawatawa dog park one afternoon and saw his bandaged arm, I wondered if there had been a dog versus human incident. Sure enough, Luna, one of the park's fastest dogs, had been in top gear and collided with Bushy, decking him and breaking his wrist. Bushy is one of the country's most famous photographers, best known for his rugby work. He comes from the West Coast, has been to war, travelled the world on merchant ships and isn't one to be laid up for long by something like a broken arm. But age is a different matter, not something that heals or can be easily countered. And in the last decade, as Bushy has tracked through his eighties, he's slowed a bit. But he's never stopped walking the hills around Wellington's south coast, where he's lived for 50 years. You'd often see him and his golden Labrador, Lottie, heading up the track at Tawatawa or along the coast towards Red Rocks of an afternoon, big raincoat over him, cracked leather boots under him, listening to Radio Sport on a transistor radio tucked into his pocket. In all weather.

He once told writer Joseph Romanos how much he loved Wellington: 'The weather's bloody lousy. How often do you hear the weather man say, "Northerlies increasing to gale force late afternoon"? But the scene changes every day, and it's magic. How many capital cities in the world are there where you can walk along the coastline to a colony of seals? If you like the outdoors and city life, Wellington's the perfect place.'

Sometimes, I'd meet him while out walking, and say, 'You're looking well, Bushy,' and he'd growl back, 'Good on ya, mate, I'll put ten bucks in your back pocket as you go past.' For a while, I didn't see Bushy, and began to wonder if his legs had given out on him. But then, one day, I spotted him toddling along the path at the dog park, two short walking sticks in his hands, a beanie keeping his ears warm. Lottie was ten paces ahead, all white fur and deep, dark eyes, pausing every now and then to check on her boss. Bushy said he was going okay, apart from his knee, which was completely buggered—bone on bone, he reckoned. He was waiting for a specialist's appointment in a few weeks, and hopefully an operation soon afterwards. He'd been booked in earlier that year to have it done, but then had to have emergency surgery for something else. Then he got pneumonia in hospital and was so sick they gave him the last rites, called his family in and said he wouldn't see dawn. But he did, and every dawn since. When the doctor asked him if there was anything he wanted, Bushy said, 'I just want to be able to go home, sit in the sun and pat my dog.'

He'd been on a strict diet since then, given up the booze and felt pretty good. The doctors had told him to keep mobile, so here he was, walking Lottie. 'Any day you wake up and can look up at the big blue sky rather than being underground in a pine overcoat is a good one,' he said. At nearly 90, Bushy was slow, but still out there, a wonderful example of just getting on with things.

'They told me to only walk on the flat,' Bushy said, with a smile and a shine in his eyes, as he planted his walking poles and set off up the hill.

DOG PARKS ARE, LIKE CIVIL society, generally places of peace and calm. But, also like society, not everyone gets along. Not everyone wants to be buddies. Not everyone believes in deference and a few rounds of courteous bum-sniffing.

In this respect, I won't pretend Cooper is an angel, or anything much approaching it. He's not a monster, but he has been known to have the odd incipient crack or two at another dog who's got too close and got in his face. I tell myself it's just the dog park hierarchy being established and reinforced. Others probably interpret it as Cooper being a bully. All I'll say is that his teeth have never drawn blood—well, not that I'm aware of. On the scale of dog ferocity, he's probably a two out of ten. Maybe three, when goaded on a really grumpy day.

There have, however, been a couple of disgraceful episodes, strangely with his mate Hamish. They've known each other since they were pups, romp happily in the long grass, tussle over sticks and shout constantly in each other's ears. But, every now and then, one of them obviously shouts something bad in the other one's ear, or one misunderstands the other one, and it's suddenly all on.

Dog fights happen with speed. Out of nothing, ferocity and attempted murder flare. What's that line from *Julius Caesar*? 'Cry havoc and let slip the dogs of war . . .' At dog parks, it's sort of the reverse. Such is the surprise and mayhem when violence breaks out that the dogs'

CRY HAVOC AND LET SLIP
THE DOGS OF WAR.

owners tend to act with sloth when the situation really demands instant intervention. The initial human reaction is to indeed cry havoc and shout at the offenders, but in truth the chances of them hearing you are minimal, given they've got a bulging-eyed aggressor snarling, 'I'm going to kill you,' an inch from their earhole. And, anyway, they hear you shouting their name with urgency all day for minor infractions, and have happily learned they can get away with ignoring it—so are they really going to bother listening and responding now, when their blood is boiling? Fat chance. So the owners shouting just adds to the noise and confusion and rarely sorts things out.

I mean, nobody likes to insert themselves into the middle of two or more dogs attempting to rip each other's faces off, but in my experience it's often the only way to prevent someone losing an eye. So, foolishly or not, I've often thrust a hopeful arm into the middle of the chaos in an attempt to grab something—a collar would be good, a handful of neck scruff is adequate, a top or bottom jaw less than ideal. It's largely a matter of luck, because the reality is that a dog fight is a blur of teeth and fur and fury. I've only been bitten once, when trying to separate a German shepherd called Kaiser and a Great Dane who had a reputation for frightening children. I should have known better and left them to it. Fortunately, the result was nothing more serious than a puncture wound to my wrist that an understanding doctor cleaned up.

When Cooper and Hamish go at it, I generally aim for Cooper and lunge into the blur, make a grab, try to lift him vertically as though he's been blasted by an ejector seat, then swing him away from Hamish, who's usually not keen to end things so hastily. Often, it's nowhere near as efficient as I planned, and I end up sprawled on the ground holding the hind leg of one or other of them, dignity disappeared, dogs still growling.

Once calm has been restored—however it happens—the pair of them sit apart in disgrace, feigning something that swings between innocence and contrition. The odd tuft of fur dangling from a chin undermines both emotions. Everyone else's pulse rates drop back into double figures, and suddenly you notice the birds singing again. There are remonstrations, lectures, threatened recriminations and an agreement that blame should probably be shared equally. Then we all head off to start the day, Cooper and Hamish trotting amiably up the path together. What was all that about?

BUT, EVERY NOW AND THEN, things get a bit more serious and a bit more real than the normal dog park scuffle. So it was with one particular dog, a lanky giant who arrived at the park some years back with his owner. One morning, Harry and Leo were bounding through an overgrown fringe of long grass when the lanky giant raced into the thick of proceedings. Some later described it as more of a pounce, but that may have had an element of re-imagination. Anyway, what followed was a shrill cry from Harry in the undergrowth. The lanky giant's owner ran down to investigate, but it was hard to know what had happened and everyone eventually went their separate ways.

It wasn't until later that morning that Barbro and Ross found Harry lying in their hallway, the fur on his flank matted with blood. Further probing revealed a large hole. Harry was rushed to the vet clinic, where he was operated on, with drains inserted and stitches secured before he was sent home, a morose little man. The lanky giant, it seemed, had taken rough and tumble to the next level.

Of course, his owner was oblivious to all this post-park aftermath. So what to do? A few of us had a chat and decided that, for the sake of park harmony, we had to inform him about what had happened. Not in an effort to ostracise or shame, but just to let him know his dog might need to be watched a bit more closely. I was somehow delegated to be the one who broached the issue, so the next time he arrived I went over and explained everything, and said that, while Harry was okay, he wouldn't be at the park for a while on account of his injuries. I expected the lanky giant's owner to be mortified and apologetic. He seemed neither; he was more dubious than anything. He'd seen no blood, he said. They'd probably fallen into the blackberries and that's how Harry had been torn, he suggested. I demurred and said that really wasn't possible, only for him to insist, 'No, you'd be surprised how that stuff can rip them when they're going fast.' At this point I knew I'd completely failed—failed at conciliation, failed at counselling, failed at delicate dog park detente—despite having spent 48 hours mulling over how best to raise it.

He walked off.

Jeremy arrived. 'How did that go?' he asked.

'Not brilliant. Not even good,' I replied. 'He reckoned Harry must have got caught up in the blackberries.'

'Blackberry bush, my arse,' Jeremy thundered. 'He's a problem.' He meant the lanky giant.

The next time I saw his owner, he asked after Harry and I tried to gently stress how it was a pretty serious injury. He generously offered to pay for Harry's vet bill, but— with an eye to future dog park interactions and wanting to suggest something positive rather than punitive for his dog—I said, 'What about having a chat with the vet about what might be best for him? Perhaps it might help if he had his nuts whopped off? That often calms them down.'

'Oh no, we're not at that stage yet,' he replied.

I wanted to say, 'Well, I think your dog might actually have reached that stage. You might be lagging behind somewhat, at the end of his leash, but if I was you I'd be doing everything I could to minimise the chance of this happening again.'

But of course I didn't say that. I was too gutless. Couldn't find the right words. I just suggested something banal like 'Maybe it might be good to think about what could be done to moderate or mitigate your dog's behaviour'.

He offered to keep his dog away from Harry, but that didn't fill me with great comfort—dogs can run far more quickly than we can catch them. At the same time, I felt awful for him. Here he was doing all the right things and trying to socialise his dog and giving him wonderful exercise, and now the lanky giant was being painted as a brute, a villainous spectre in the undergrowth. I gave up my attempted intercession, figuring I wasn't the park police-man and these things would have to sort themselves out.

Then, on a routine visit to our vet, Pete, who's wonder-fully common sense about all things dog, I asked what he would do. He enquired what breed the dog was and, when I said he was a Bouvier des Flandres, Pete jerked his head back. He said he'd witnessed a friend's dog get mauled by one of them; he was adamant they were dangerous and unpredictable and insisted they should be banned, along with the likes of Dogo Argentinos. Pete suggested we should be blunt and insist that the lanky giant needed to be kept on a lead—because Pete was positive he would attack something small and fluffy again, and possibly kill them. A muzzle would be a useful foil, but it wouldn't stop his intimidating behaviour, Pete said. And neutering him probably wouldn't prevent his attacks either, because it was learned behaviour by now.

I felt slightly vindicated in my concerns, and bolstered in the belief it hadn't been a roving blackberry cane that had caused Harry's wound. At the same time, I also felt deflated by the thought that the lanky giant, purely due to his breeding, might be a lost cause. He had a lot of years to live, and I wanted them to be happy ones. I walked out of the vet's, with Pete's sobering message in my head, feeling we were back to square one with the lanky giant, reliant on some behavioural miracle.

I'm not entirely sure whether this happened, though, because his owner took the initiative and took to walking him elsewhere. Occasionally, I'd see them wandering up the road near their house, the lanky giant tethered and his owner looking unenthused. I felt a little guilty that they perhaps didn't feel comfortable or welcome at the park any more, but if I'm honest there was also a sense of relief. You don't walk your dog to be on edge. Scanning the approaches to the dog park for possible marauders is a joyless vigil. The rest of life can be an anxious enough pursuit without dog walks being fretful too.

THE AWFUL AND FRUSTRATING THING is that sometimes, no matter what you do or how much effort you put in, some dogs just go bad—and then go from bad to bastard.

When we first got Cooper, we would take him to

Tawatawa dog park in the afternoons, where there were a bunch of other pups finding their feet in the world and learning how it worked. Gin came to the park with Jake, the shoe eater, who was a big boy of mixed origin. Perhaps he came to believe his size entitled him to be the boss of the park. Perhaps something frightful had gone on before Gin got him. Whatever it was, Jake started attacking other dogs out of the blue. Gin tried a couple of muzzles, but Jake quickly worked out how to get them off. So, in the end, she would walk Jake in the late evening, when there were no other dogs around, two sad silhouettes circling the park's perimeter at dusk. Poor Gin. She looked so disconsolate and frustrated, which was understandable given she'd done everything they tell you to do with your new dog.

'I was taking him to puppy preschool before he was even three months old,' she said.

Plus, just like Cooper and the rest of the gang, Jake'd had brilliant socialisation time twice a day, growing up at the park with dozens of other dogs.

'I'm trying a few things with him, but I think it's time to call in a dog whisperer person,' she said, with resignation, one time.

'Definitely,' I replied. 'Nothing to lose.'

'He's just a bastard,' Gin continued. 'But, the thing is, at home he's a perfect dog, just lies down quietly.'

I didn't know what to say. So I didn't try.

But sometimes, Jake's behaviour came up in conversation, no matter how discreet everyone tried to be.

'Oh, you all missed what happened up here last night,' a chatty woman announced one evening, as she arrived at a semicircle of us standing around. 'Huge fight.'

She then went on to describe an all-in, all-on affray, with the pitiful wailings of the small-dog victim echoing around Tawatawa's bushy amphitheatre. She'd heard the commotion from the upper track and arrived just in time to see the aftermath—and the wounds. Essential park gossip imparted, the woman tottered off towards her car, twin terriers at heel.

'Guess what. You know who that was?' said Gin, her voice sinking somewhere between depression and desperation. 'Jake.'

Sure enough, the night before, despite being on the lead, Jake had ripped away from Gin and ripped into another dog. Luckily, a fellow dog walker, Dave, had intervened, eventually headbutting Jake in order to separate the dogs. Don't ask me exactly how that worked, but Gin said Dave was left holding his nose, eyes streaming and his glasses lost somewhere in the mud.

Poor, poor Gin. As if it wasn't bad enough dealing with Jake's behaviour, she had to hear it repeated by strangers and know it was the chatter of the dog park. And it's an awful feeling when you've got the bad dog, the misfit bully, but you just don't know why.

There's that truism that there are no bad dogs, only bad owners—and, generally, that would be right. But Gin was the furthest from a bad owner you could get. And it's not just her, either; I've seen some of the most devoted and loving owners flummoxed by their dog's behaviour. Human reasoning counts for little in such situations. Dogs may be man's best friend, but they're still a separate species.

Oh yes, there are animal experts and behaviourists and dog gurus who I'm sure would make a difference with most dogs if given time, but they'd have their work cut out with some of the dogs I've come across. You know all those dog programmes on TV, where they show incredible turnarounds in troublesome dogs or homeless mongrels becoming furred prodigies? I have to wonder whether they ever show you the failures, all the purebred basket cases who didn't respond to training and likely bit someone's leg off-camera. It's reality TV, and the reality is that some dogs don't make it.

And should we be surprised by this? Hardly. As humans, we can't even cure our own ills or solve the world's problems, most of which we've created—and we speak the same language.

OF COURSE, BITING OTHER DOGS at the park is one thing. Biting other people's pets at their own home is in another, slightly more criminal league. When Roger turned up at the park one morning looking glum and grim, we soon discovered there was good reason. The day before, his big black poodle, Aggie, had got out the gate, and snuck into their neighbours' place, where there were two pet rabbits.

The rabbits had been outside, tied to a tree in the garden, enjoying the fresh air and plentiful grass. Roger noticed the open gate, noticed Aggie was missing, and went next door on a hunch. When the neighbour came out, Roger asked if he could check if Aggie was there, and they went around the back of the house. Sure enough, there was Aggie, with one dead rabbit in front of her. Remarkably, the neighbour went, 'Oh, well. We've got another one over there.'

But Aggie had already got that one too.

Tethered, they were easy pickings. Faced with two disembowelled rabbits, a grieving neighbour and a guilty dog, what do you say? 'I'll buy you a couple more,' hardly cuts it.

LEST IT BE ASSUMED COOPER is entirely without fault or the ability to cause humiliation, the events of a 2017 Christmas party should prove that he, like any dog, will disgrace you royally and publicly at some stage. Hobbs's owners, Briar and Jan, had invited a bunch of us out for a barbecue at their Whitby home, including several dog park acquaintances and five dogs in total. The doors were open, nibbles were being nibbled, crumbs were being dropped, balls were being chewed and chased out on the lawn, and all the dogs were in high festive spirits, going full tilt with lolling tongues and big smiles.

I was inside when I heard shrieks of surprise and laughter from beyond the ranchsliders—but not quite the laughter of a really good time or a cracking joke. Then I saw Gary enter from the garden, the bottom of one trouser leg suspiciously darkened—by dog piss, it transpired. It also transpired that Cooper was responsible. He'd simply sauntered up to Gary out of the blue and merrily lifted his leg on him. Standing by the fence, gazing at progress on Transmission Gully's new highway far below, it's possible Gary's leg resembled a fence post. Gary might have just been in the wrong place at the wrong time—well, that much is inarguable. Or perhaps Cooper just forgot the rules of polite society, specifically the bit that says pissing on people is well out of order any time, but especially at Christmas parties.

Gary tried to put his best peace-and-goodwill-to-man-and-beast-at-Christmas look on his face, but he was understandably annoyed. You go to a party and you get pissed on before the barbie is even ready, and it's not as if you've thought of this eventuality and brought a change of trousers. Or shoes. Oh yes, Cooper's blithe jet stream had also soaked one of Gary's leather loafers. Luckily, Briar's father was staying the night and had a spare pair of shorts, which he donated to Gary for the rest of the evening. But I think Gary went barefoot after that.

Again, it's not the kind of dog offence you can truly make light of—'Oh, aren't they funny things . . .' And it's not the kind of felony an apology truly makes amends for. An offer to pay for dry-cleaning seems both inadequate for the embarrassment, and yet also a potential over-reach. Mentioning that Cooper has never done anything like this before will be seen as fatuous excusing. So what can you do, other than sit there ashamed, smiling wanly as the inevitable jokes swirl and wash over you, hoping the conversation moves on quickly?

Cooper felt none of these things, of course. He wheeled with his mates and dashed in and out for quick pats. He snuffled for sausage scraps, and rehydrated himself from the water bowl. His tail wagged all night long. It was the best Christmas party ever.

9.
The jobs we give them

When wolves crept from the forest's fringe 30,000 years ago, edged closer to humans' campfires and eventually became domesticated and reliant on us, they probably didn't contemplate the quid pro quo of the deal. In return for food and warmth and shelter and companionship, they have over the years been corralled into all manner of responsibilities and jobs. They've been crucial allies in hunting, and still are today—'Go latch on to the scary pig and hold him till I get there . . .' 'Go swim out into the icy pond and fetch the duck I've just winged . . .' They find lost trampers and rescue people from avalanches, they track rare birds for conservationists, they apprehend evildoers for the police, they sniff out contraband for customs agents, they sit for hour after tedious hour with beggars, toying with our sympathy, they're lifelong companions for the blind and anxious, they detect cancer and predict epileptic seizures.

Cooper, meanwhile, fetches the paper. It's his single

duty, the one expectation we have of him, beyond being moderately well behaved. Each morning, when we get up, we'll open the door and he shoots out in search of *The Dominion Post*, wrapped and rolled securely in plastic, somewhere on our property. It's a bit of a crapshoot—the person who flings it from the delivery car before dawn has an unreliable arm and aim. Sometimes, the paper is on the hedge; sometimes, on the garage roof; sometimes, well up the path; sometimes, somehow wedged behind a downpipe or lodged behind the recycling bin. This uncertainty adds to Cooper's task, but to be fair the paper is often lying near the door on our front deck, requiring him to take only a few paces to retrieve it, then proudly trot back inside, tail in the air, the day's headlines dangling from his mouth.

For such a Herculean workload he receives two small biscuits as a reward, his tail flicking in excited expectation as he sits on the mat and waits for us to retrieve them from an ice-cream container in the kitchen. Such is the routine, and such is the extent of Cooper's working day. From then on, it's pure indulgence—walks, sleeping, barking at the postie, a bone at lunchtime, barking at the neighbour's car, another walk, more sleeping, more eating, all interspersed with being scratched around his ears. Hardship is not a word I reach for when reflecting on Cooper's life.

But for thousands of his ilk the working day and routine is quite different. My last two dogs—Cas and now

Cooper—have been huntaways, the distinctly New Zealand dog bred to be a farmer's foil and best mate. Black and tan with the odd splash of white, their on-farm skill is in the way they drive sheep by barking from behind them. It might seem simple, until you factor in the obtuse unpredictability of sheep, that frustrating mix of stupidity and malevolence. Each and every one of those sheep has the potential to be a complete shit. Congregate them in mobs of hundreds or more and the likelihood of mayhem is enormous—almost guaranteed. Thus, any dog who's going to control them has to possess an incredible mix of intelligence and athleticism, stealth and strength, guile and endurance.

Genuine huntaways are big beasts, standing up to your thigh, with heads half the size of a horse's and paws that wouldn't be amiss on grizzly bear cubs. Neither of my huntaways have been that size—probably diluted versions, the bastardised results of farmyard accidents. Cas came from a farm, part of an unwanted litter that was going to be drowned until the farmer's teenage daughter pleaded for a chance to find the pups homes and put an ad in the paper. We got the last one.

Cooper was probably from a farm, probably part of another unintended litter and probably dumped by the gutless prick of an owner. He was found wandering in a Northland forest, a tiny bewildered pup, and taken to the SPCA.

Neither of them ever did a day's real work. Any time

spent in rural paddocks during their cosseted lives has been extremely limited, any random brush with sheep a study in confusion on both sides: the dogs perplexed by such strange-looking woolly dogs, and the sheep bemused by such half-witted dogs with no voice.

However, I always dreamed that all Cas and Cooper needed was a bit of training and they'd become star working dogs, that their genetics and the intelligence I perceived in them would make them prized assets to any farmer. What they dreamed of was entirely different, I imagine, and I doubt there were any sheep in whatever floated through their subconscious as they twitched and whimpered while dozing away their days of idle luxury. The closest they came to a Corriedale or a Romney were the sheepskins that lined their indulgent beds.

Well, that's not entirely true. Cooper did sort of take part in the Shepherds Shemozzle in Hunterville one year, part of the town's annual huntaway festival. It's a riotous race, where shepherds and others run with their dogs over a short but punishing course, wheezing up hills, careering down mudslides, then negotiate an array of undignified and unlikeable obstacles down the town's main street. All this while dressed in an old sack. Nikki was writing a story about it and thought it would be fun to see how Cooper the townie huntaway acquitted himself. Not very well was the answer. We didn't think it would be a good idea to actually enter Cooper in the race, so the organisers instead let Nikki run over much of the course and try some of the obstacles. Cooper loved running beside Nikki as she ploughed through the swamp. He loved it so much that he found a stick and decided this would be a great place to play fetch, so dropped the stick at Nikki's feet. He whizzed down the mudslide, easily beating Nikki to the filthy pond at the bottom.

But, once back on the course in Hunterville, he wasn't having a bar of being conveyed in a wheelbarrow, and had to be coaxed through the sack tunnel. It was all captured on video for *Stuff* as part of Nikki's story. It's probably still online. Please don't look at it. It's humiliating for Cooper, as well as for Nikki and me, who've turned a proud dog of the backcountry into a city softie. Suffice to say, he would be a complete liability if let loose on a farm.

LIKE MANY, I GREW UP with sheepdog trialling on TV, the edge-of-the-seat action of *A Dog's Show* on Sundays balanced by droll commentary from John Gordon. Visitors to New Zealand were always amazed such an obscure activity could have been wrangled into such popular entertainment. And not just entertainment for rural folk who understood the rules and details of the sport, but also for city-dwellers whose only connection with the countryside was as ultimate consumers, the urbanites at the end of a food chain that began hundreds of miles away up some remote valley in a brutal hill-block. Dog trialling on TV might seem an utter anachronism nowadays, but I challenge you to watch an old episode on YouTube and not be caught up in the drama or be amazed by John Gordon's lexicon of understatements.

On account of my nostalgia for the days of *A Dog's Show*, my admiration for the skill involved and my fondness for farm dogs, I'd always wanted to attend the national sheepdog trials and write a story about it. My editor at *North & South* indulged my enthusiasm, and the perfect opportunity arose in mid-2015. I'd just spent two months in court, covering the retrial of Mark Lundy, who was accused of murdering his wife and seven-year-old daughter; the best part of summer disappearing as we sat in Wellington's High Court revisiting the horrors of their deaths time and again from endless angles and countless witnesses. When the jury returned and the verdict was given, we emerged into short days and sun with scant warmth, autumn already well underway. After weeks of grimness, I craved something other than murder. Taihape and the country's premier dog-trialling contest offered an unlikely but ideal antidote.

My road to the championships had actually been a long one, one that began the previous year with a chance meeting. In the run-up to the 2014 election, I'd spent a week driving from Auckland to Wellington tracing then-Prime Minister John Key's weekly route from his

Parnell home to Parliament, gauging the public's views on his popularity. Heading south from Taihape early one morning, I noticed a sign on a fence beside State Highway 2 advertising Tux dog biscuits and pointing to the annual Ohingaiti District Collie Club dog trials up a side road. This seemed like the perfect place to hear the truly rural voice, authentic hinterland views rooted in ryegrass and Red Bands, I thought, so I turned off the highway.

I was early for the trials, but was greeted by the organisers, who ushered me in to the clubrooms, sat me down in front of a plate of warm date scones, butter sinking deliciously into them, and slid a cup of tea in front of me, its steam unfurling slowly upwards into the midwinter sunshine. I chatted politics with men who'd decorously left their dew-coated gumboots at the door, and women who had decades of experience readying mammoth morning teas.

But, truth be told, it was dogs I wanted to talk about. So, when Paul Evans introduced himself and said he was organising the national championships the following year, I knew that Tux sign that had caught my eye on the main road had been serendipity. Paul was a big man with big plans for what they were going to lay on for the country's top dog triallists. I liked him immediately, and we kept in touch over the following year and made plans for me to spend several days covering the event.

By the time the championships rolled around and

I arrived in Taihape, May frosts had turned the trial grounds hard as pig iron. The competitors stood in clusters, stamping their feet and rubbing their hands to eke out any warmth. I wore my Red Bands, but felt like an idiot interloper from the city, an urban imposter in a world of people who were rugged, resourceful and had dogs who slept outside. I vowed not to mention that I too owned a huntaway, but one who slept in a wicker basket lined with a sheepskin and polar fleece and had blankets draped over him on cold nights.

But, the competitors were wonderful and welcoming and they patiently explained how each event worked, what the judges looked for and what the dogs should and shouldn't do. (They should never sniff—that shows they're not concentrating. They should never pee while on the course, and can only nip a sheep if it's charging them—and then only on the head.) They also outlined the rules triallists must adhere to. (No swearing on the course, no sticks longer than a metre, no collars on dogs, and no 'objectionable' dogs—meaning bitches on heat—on the grounds.)

There are four events at sheepdog trials: two heading events, and two huntaway events called hunts. The long head sees dogs run up a steep hillside and bring three sheep back to a ring, where the sheep must be held still. In the short head and yard, the dog travels a smaller distance to get the sheep, but once on the flat they must drive the sheep through a hurdle and into a pen. In both these classes, the dogs use their eyes and movement to shift the sheep.

In the hunts, the dogs bark, forcing sheep directly up a hillside in the straight hunt, and through sets of markers in the zigzag hunt.

In all events, the top seven dogs from the first round run off for the trophies.

The 2015 event was being held about fifteen minutes' drive from Taihape's township, up a road that sees few visitors, amid a pitiless span of Rangitikei hill country. The land was striated with slips, and full of guts and gullies—tough country that was tough on dogs. In one corner stood the Moawhango Collie Club shed, its honours board speaking of past championships, legendary men, and dogs inscribed into rural lore. Spot, Speed, Smoke. Flame, Blaze, Haze. Wag, Toss, Lass. Beside it were photos stretching back more than a century. In the old days, triallists dressed up, the men wearing suits, hats and buttonholes. A programme from the club's twenty-fourth annual trials in 1926 noted competition would be followed by a dance at Mr Hakopa's hall. 'Good music, good floor, good supper, Dash's orchestra. Non-members 5 shillings. Ladies free.'

Paul Evans and his committee members knew they had tradition to follow and standards to uphold. They intended to put on the best championships ever. But there were limits to ceremony nowadays—nobody wore a suit or buttonhole any more, and hats were restricted to beanies emblazoned with various rural suppliers' logos. A shearing gang was providing the food: plenty of meat and potatoes and gravy. 'You can't go up that hill on a cabbage and a carrot, mate,' said cook Rudy Lewis, hovering over a hot plate. The odd loose dog sniffed hopefully around the back of the food tent, then wandered off to splash a truck tyre.

Nearly 300 competitors with 500 dogs had qualified for the week-long championships, following months of provincial trials. They came from Southland to Northland, some with reputations and a host of previous titles, while others were nervous rookies. All had lean dogs whose noses poked from dog boxes or the back of utes, sniffing a winter breeze sprinkled with sheep shit and anticipation.

Success in dog trialling is part skill, part luck. The exact proportion of each is something discussed at length. Some reckon luck is 10 per cent; others estimate it's double or even treble that. But one thing everyone agrees on is that if the sheep are wilful, flighty or fresh you won't win—and that factor is a pure lottery.

When it comes to the dogs, half a step here, six inches there—the smallest things—can be the difference between the perfect manoeuvre and complete ovine chaos, between honours and heartbreak. Some dogs respond like robots to their owner's commands one day, then like distracted

A GOOD DOG.

delinquents the next. There's no accounting for mood, and no concession for an off day.

A lot comes down to breeding, just like horses. Competitors trace their dogs' lineage back generations, and careful negotiations take place over ute bonnets as they discuss who they're going to mate their dogs with to improve their bloodline and chances. Top dogs can fetch well over $10,000. It's a fickle and frustrating sport. While kennel clubs prize beauty, sheepdog trials are all about performance.

Forbes Minto from Dannevirke had been coming to these championships for years and always driven home luckless. This time, he'd waited five bitter days to compete in the short head with his dog, Tan, and was the second to last to run out of 250 competitors. All that waiting and watching, the 77-year-old with a greenstone whistle around his neck, and a stick made from lancewood and deer antler at his side. But, when Tan started, he went way off course, way out right, looking for imaginary sheep in a neighbouring gully. All that anticipation and anxiety—it was all over in 20 seconds, as Minto called Tan in, and wandered back to his ute. 'Nah, not that time,' he shrugged as Tan leaped in, and Minto flicked up the tailgate.

Others got much closer before their hopes vanished with an unfortunate misstep or on account of a single sheep's whim. Whangarei's Allen Nisbet and his dog, Maggie, were having a good run in the short head, the lambs sedately driven up to the final pen. But, as Nisbet held the gate open and Maggie eyeballed the sheep, one broke and the others scattered in solidarity. Nisbet knew the game was over and called Maggie in, patting her generously on the flank. 'Whatever,' he smiled as he trudged off. 'Been there a thousand times.'

On the dog-trialling ground, it's a small step between elation and deflation.

THE QUARDLE AND CACKLE OF magpies in the treetops mixed with shrill shepherds' whistles in the valley, as the finalists for each event were gradually found. On the huntaway course, the tinkle of spectators' Tui bottles provided a descant to the throaty bark of the dogs.

Paul Cole stood to one side, as the finalists for the zigzag hunt readied themselves and their dogs. After the first run, Cole and his dog, Quid, were leading, following a near-perfect 98-point run. And given he had previously won national titles, smart money was on Cole to stay in front. With a cigarette stuck to his bottom lip, smoke rising and yellowing his drooping grey moustache at the tips, he was someone I desperately wanted to photograph for my story. But the look on his face clearly said, 'Don't try it. Piss off.'

I decided to ignore both his look and my better judgement. Sidling over, I introduced myself and said I was writing a story about the championships. As I did so, I instinctively reached down to pat Quid.

'Don't touch the dog,' Cole growled, the menace in his message uncamouflaged.

I'd barely touched Quid's head, scarcely ruffled a hair. Cole saw things differently and seemed to regard me as a molester. It was as if he thought pats were for townie triflers, and would corrupt Quid into a life of ease and disobedience.

I'd heard that admonition before. 'Don't touch the dog,' ordered the customs officer at Auckland International Airport, as the Labrador sniffed my crotch and sat down directly in front of me. I'd just collected my bag from the carousel after a week in India, and imagined a heady potpourri of scents was probably being picked up by Rover the drugs dog. Cardamom, saffron, chilli, masala— you name it, it was undoubtedly there somewhere. Rover's handler obviously had different ideas—ideas of heroin and hashish. 'Don't touch the dog,' he repeated, as Rover remained rooted in my way. He then asked me to go into an area that might as well have been signposted 'suspected drug mules and other contraband smugglers', while everyone else chose between green or red lanes. 'That's the best reaction he's ever given,' Rover's handler whispered to a colleague behind me as I was marched into the interrogation area, my mind whirling about what someone may have concealed in my bag without my knowledge.

They leave you sitting there for some time, watching from the other side of one-way glass, your bag unopened in front of you, as if you're meant to be shamed by it and all the wickedness that you've foolishly tried to secrete in its seams, and then collapse, crying and confessing. Eventually, a bald man with a bad attitude emerged and, without pleasantries, asked me where I'd come from and when the last time was that I'd used drugs. Not 'Have you used drugs?' but the blunt assumption you must be an addict if you've ended up in this part of the arrivals hall. The exaggerated snap of latex on his wrists as he donned gloves was something I was sure he'd practised for effect. He rummaged and poked, unzipped and probed. Then, with B-movie theatricality, he swabbed the inside of my bag and announced he was going to test it. Of course he was.

And of course it came back blank, inert, harmless, innocent. The bald customs man looked slightly perplexed and quite pissed off. There were no apologies for delaying me, or for his rote and baseless accusations. I repacked my bag and exited, worrying all the while that Rover was getting his arse kicked out the back for wasting everyone's time.

Cole's order to not touch the dog was delivered with the same stern urgency as that of the customs officer. It left no room for confusion or even a quick scratch of Quid's ears. After that blunder, that careless ignoring of etiquette, there was no hope of Cole warming to me, no chance of a wry quote, let alone a photo. I had, quite simply, breached protocol and buggered things up.

And, when Cole and Quid stepped into the starting area, it went to crap for them as sheep scattered, oblivious to Quid's barks and Cole's commands. In the end, they scored 89 out of 100 for their run—the lowest score of the seven finalists—and plummeted from first to last place. I looked across at them after they'd finished and Cole returned my glance with a glare, no doubt blaming me for diverting his dog with affection. Bloody townies—just bloody trouble. Piss off.

I slunk away and found the winner, who was so thrilled, so cock-a-hoop, he didn't care how many pats I gave his dog.

IT'S DIFFICULT TO OVERSTATE HOW esteemed a national sheepdog trialling title is. There is prize money and there is a silver platter, but the thing competitors value most is the green tie you are presented with, which identifies you as one of a small and select club who have won at the nationals. That green tie was something each of the seven finalists in the long head event thought about as they made their way to the grounds on the championship's last day. To get to the last round was remarkable in itself; to win would be extraordinary.

Dawn had unveiled another brute of a frost, mud cast into concrete and water troughs iced solid. The leader after the first round was Merv Williams with Showman. Andy Clark, a painter from Darfield who had to drive nearly an hour from home to find hills to practise on, was half a point back; his dog, Lady, now nine and probably having her last run at the nationals. Gathered to one side, waiting for the sun to slide over the ridge and thaw the ground around them, were the next three places—Guy Peacock, Graham Wellington and Ian McKinnon. Fewer than two points separated the top five.

McKinnon stood shivering. Frosts were unfamiliar in Dargaville, where he ran a 240-hectare beef farm and his wife was a midwife, but it was probably nerves that had him shaking. All the other competitors had been in finals before and three had won titles, but this was McKinnon's first ever run-off.

Wellington had won this event in 2005 with the grandmother of his current dog, Rachael, but still doubted himself, admitting he didn't handle the pressure well. Rachael snuggled into him, her wet nose seeking his dangling hand. Wellington had named her after his granddaughter, who used to be interested in his dogs. 'But now she's a teenager, and she's more interested in bands and boys and things like that than she is in dog trials and grandfathers,' he mourned.

At eight o'clock, the first competitor, McKinnon, strode

to the mark and set Tess loose into an amphitheatre of hills. Their run was superb, and onlookers muttered words like 'outstanding'.

And when Williams had a bad one, and the sheep inexplicably broke at the top of the course for Wellington, and Clark produced only a fair performance, it seemed the new boy, McKinnon, was on the cusp of a sizeable upset. Only one pair remained, Guy Peacock and Falcon.

It had been a strange week for Peacock. He'd started poorly, his first runs in snow and hail, and his results had been equally dismal. However, things had improved in the last two days, and he'd finished third in the straight hunt with his huntaway, Tom, and now reached the long head final with Falcon. But, during the week, Peacock had also caught wind that an old friend and fellow dog triallist, Fred McDougal, had died, aged 88. Just dropped dead on his wee block out of Waipukurau. Nearly 20 years before, when Peacock was starting life as a shepherd, McDougal had taken him under his wing on Tautane Station and taught him about dogs and life on the hills. 'We'd go to a dog trial, and he'd say, "We'll get old-fashioned drunk, shall we?"' recalled Peacock. 'And I'd say, "You get old-fashioned drunk, and I'll get us home."'

He'd last seen McDougal in February at the Tautane trials. 'He was pretty beat up, but he got up and got there and still had a smile on his face and run his dog on the long head. He was a good old mate.'

So, as he'd driven to Moawhango for the run-off that morning, Peacock had thought to himself, *I'll do this one for you, Freddy.*

At 38, Peacock was one of the younger competitors. But Falcon was aging—eight now, with a bung hip and largely blind in one eye, though still 'pretty honest', Peacock reckoned. They'd been a good team for a while, but they'd never won a national title—a second and a third their best efforts. This year, Peacock noticed Falcon had lost that turn of speed that drove him up the hills. At the start of the week, Peacock had whispered in his dog's ear that, if he did well, he'd retire him at the trial's end. So this was his last shot at a title, and everything started perfectly when Peacock set him off.

Falcon flew up the course, up a vicious 500-metre slope, curved around behind the sheep, then suddenly stopped and crouched flat, 20 metres above them, his course replicating the shape of a question mark, until he was just a distant black dot to the spectators far below. Then he silently coaxed the sheep down, only Peacock making any sound, whistling and shouting instructions across the still morning.

Each competitor has sixteen minutes to complete the course, which seems plenty, but the sheep were touchy and Falcon had to work hard to keep them going straight, which ate up time. And, when he finally got them to the flats, the sheep just didn't want to move, almost inching their way across the final 300 metres as Falcon slipped this way and that behind them, and seconds slipped away.

Peacock repeatedly checked his watch: two minutes, one and a half-minutes, one minute . . .

With twelve seconds remaining, Peacock took one last glance at his watch. The sheep still weren't in the ring, and if he went even a second over time he'd automatically finish last.

The sheep crept forward into the ring, and Falcon darted around them, but as he did the lead sheep flinched and they started to bolt.

'Steady, Falc! Steady, Falc! Steady . . . Steady . . . STEADY, FALC!' Peacock yelled.

In a plywood hut just behind them, judge's clerk Diana Davis looked at the official stopwatch and began counting down the remaining seconds. 'Ten . . . nine . . . eight . . .'

Peacock frantically tried to steady the sheep in the ring and get Falcon lined up on the other side. Falcon froze, the sheep stopped, Peacock spread his arms to show he was done and the judge shouted 'time'. There were four seconds left.

Peacock tipped his face to the sky and heaved a giant sigh as he walked from the ring. Waiting for him were wife Lisa, their two boys, Harry and George, and his parents. His mum, Vivienne, wearing gumboots covered with multicoloured peace symbols, had been there all week, driving through a snowstorm to get to the trials from her

Waipukurau home. Peacock was exhausted and, cradling a bottle of energy drink, admitted it was the tensest run he'd ever had at a dog trial. 'Definitely. Absolutely,' he sputtered, an overflow of adrenaline rendering his speech a series of staccato sentences.

An hour later, the results were posted at the event headquarters. Peacock and Falcon had won by 0.8 points from McKinnon, with Clark third, followed by Williams and Wellington. Just three points covered all of them.

There's no exultation at events like this and little emotion. But there was no doubt Peacock was thrilled to have won, stoked that Falcon could bow out a national champion.

He drank a whisky in memory of Fred McDougal, said bye to his parents, who were heading back to Hawke's Bay, then got ready to go home himself, to the 3,000-hectare station he managed in the Turakina Valley on the other side of Taihape, where he'd be mustering sheep with horses and dogs on big hill country tomorrow. Falcon would be there alongside him.

Right now, though, Falcon was nowhere to be seen.

'Wayleggo, Falc!' Peacock yelled. 'WAYLEGGO, FALC!'

And, from the far corner of a broad paddock, in a blur of black and white, grace and obedience, the 'pretty honest' dog came streaking back to Peacock's side.

10.

The ways we say goodbye to them

One day, not too far into the future, Cooper is going to break Nikki's heart. It may be sudden, it may be a gradual process of sadness and mixed memories, but it will happen. All dogs die. That they live such a short time compared to us seems unjust, and condemns a dog owner to several such traumas in their life. Unlike other parts of owning a dog, it never gets any easier. The oldest dog ever was Bluey, an Australian cattle dog who was 29 when he died, but most dogs won't make even half of that.

When Cooper dies, it will be Nikki's first experience of such searing loss. It will also be my worst dog experience. Our first family dog, Sandy, died when I was fifteen and I dug the hole in the garden to bury him. I hope something flourished from that patch of backyard Blenheim.

To my shame and regret, the next two dogs in my life died without me being there. I was overseas, and others had to deal with the heartbreak and hole-digging. When I left for my OE at the end of the 1980s, I knew I probably wouldn't see Gyp again—the dog my mum and I had got after Sandy. I remember my last night staying with Mum before going overseas, lying with Gyp on the carpet in the lounge at her place, tickling him. I didn't want to go to bed, didn't want to end that last interaction. About 1 a.m. Mum got up, wondering where I was, saw us dozing there, and gently said, 'Try to get some sleep.' I was well past the age where she dictated what time I went to bed, but she instinctively knew exactly how I was feeling. When I drove off the next day, I couldn't speak for a long time, guilt, grief and the effort not to let the tears that were blurring my view overflow down my face.

Three years later, I was in Canada when I found out Gyp had died. We'd arrived at a friend's place, where I'd told my family to send letters for us to collect. Clutching a bundle of mail, an asterisked note in tiny letters on a postcard from one of my sisters caught my eye and told me what I'd been expecting: 'So sorry to hear about Gyp.' I figured it could only mean one thing. A letter from Mum in the same bundle confirmed everything.

He was thirteen, and in old age had become frightened by small things. The sound of stones flicking up under the car on gravel roads would send him, mad with terror, diving into the passenger's footwell. But he remained a good and loving dog, a bitzer with heart and character, even as his energy gradually waned. Mum had to dig the hole in her garden for Gyp, under the bushes where he'd lie in summer, grappling with a bone he'd resurrected from some hidden spot along the neighbour's fence line.

When I finally got home several years later, the pilgrimage from Mum's back door to his grave, marked with a large stone, was a short one. All I could whisper to Gyp was that I was sorry I hadn't been there at the last. But then, I'd been away for much of his life, after leaving home for university, and then working around the country. I'd been an intermittent part of his existence. But, of course, he'd been a constant, crucial part of mine, no matter how far away I'd been.

My next dog, Cas, was a constant part of my daily life for her first six years. Then circumstances changed, a relationship faltered, I ended up overseas again and Cas became part of my sister's family. When I returned to New Zealand, it was decided Cas should stay where she was—she had a wonderful life there, and it was deemed fairer on her and on my sister's kids, who'd grown fond of her, that the status quo should continue. It wasn't easy, it wasn't how I'd hoped things would work out at all, but it's just how it was. And I had to accept it was my life decisions that had largely resulted in the situation. I'd look after Cas during some holidays, and that was great, but of course I knew I couldn't ever let myself think of her as *my* dog again—although deep down I did.

The last holidays I cared for her, I sort of knew I wouldn't ever see her again. I was headed overseas once more and so I whispered goodbyes into her ear, told her how much I loved her, forever, and how special she'd always be. Then, again, I drove off feeling shit, feeling like an utter shit.

Four months later, in Panama, I got another letter from my mum like the one in Canada, explaining that Cas, aged twelve, had suffered something similar to a stroke, fallen unconscious and finally stopped breathing a few hours later. It had been quick and painless, Mum insisted. I didn't know if this was the complete truth, or a convenient précis, a modified version intended to soothe me. It seemed a little too simple, and in my experience, the death of a dog rarely was. But despite my reservations, I was never brave enough to ask Mum exactly what had happened or press others who might know the truth. This time, my teenage nephew dug the hole, under some trees in the far corner of my sister's section, then cradled Cas and laid her down. Again, I'd been spared the final anguish.

There were years of happy memories, pages of photos attesting to that fact, and endless guilt once more that I'd effectively abandoned my dog at the end.

So with Cooper I want to be there whenever that end might be. I say that with determination now, but also awareness that sometimes unexpected events derail such vows. But I hope I am there, adding any succour I can, stroking his head, telling him I love him, trying not to dissolve.

ONE OF THE SADDEST THINGS I think I've ever seen was a small vignette as I turned the corner to the supermarket in Wellington's Island Bay one morning. Beside the supermarket is the vet clinic we go to. And across the road from it stood three people in tears, clutching an empty dog collar, a limp lead and each other. In the instant it took to pass them, you knew the whole story, the whole horrid series of events, from the first bad news from the vet, to that morning's impossible decisions and heartbreak. Bereft on a suburban street corner, they stood there not knowing what to do next.

Because what do you do?

You return home, and the emptiness overwhelms you. Just where are you meant to put that collar and lead now? What do you do with that remaining half-bag of dog biscuits? Save it in case you get another dog? Or is that just ghastly economy? Everything stares back at you: their water bowl, their bed, their hairs that you'll notice for months afterwards, woven into your clothes and imbedded in the furniture. Each thing accuses you to some measure as to whether you made the right decision, and whether the time was truly right.

There are all those other things that change too, the smallest things that redefine your dogless life, such as how common phrases disappear from your vocabulary. You hardly ever get to say 'good boy' again—there's no reason. There's no boy any more.

The loss is even more brutal when your dog dies young. I met Cody, a fantastic Department of Conservation ranger in Twizel, when I was doing a story about the plight of one of our rarest birds, the kakī (black stilt). They live in the Tasman Valley down from Aoraki Mount Cook, and at that time there were fewer than 100 adult kakī in total.

Cody had a dog called Jazz, who he'd trained to find kakī nests, which were devilishly camouflaged among the riverbed's stones, and her contribution to saving the species was inestimable. Not long after I'd visited, Cody sent me a text saying, 'I've had to put my best mate Jazz down today. I'm a fucking wreck if I'm being honest.' Jazz had been battling an autoimmune disease that initially attacked her tear ducts. Then it started spreading elsewhere, and Cody was left with the most horrible of decisions. 'Did all I could, but had to pack it in,' he wrote. 'Six years old, all that work put in, and she was at her peak. Goodnatured thing too. Would have been easier if she had been a bit of an arsehole.'

AT THE END OF 2014, Grahame Sydney sent me an email. I'd written a feature on him a few months earlier because he had a new book coming out that looked back at his life and career, and I'd spent several days at his home in Central Otago interviewing him. During that time, we'd often taken his two dogs walking and I'd particularly fallen for his three-legged huntaway, Gyp. She'd been a working dog for a farmer up the road, but after an accident she lost her leg and became largely confined to her kennel. Grahame and his wife, Fi, had asked if they could adopt her, so she came to live with them and had been there for several years. But, when I was with them, Gyp was becoming physically limited, unable to keep up on walks, just as happy to stay in Grahame's truck. She was just getting old.

'Since you shared our delight in the dogs here at home,' Grahame wrote in his email, 'I thought you should know that yesterday we said our final goodbye to Gyp, our much-loved three-legged old farm orphan. Fi found her early in the morning, unable to move and breathing very shallow. A rapid trip to the vet in Alex[andra] revealed she had a large tumour on the spleen, which was bleeding, and X-rays showed further small tumours scattered about her lungs and system. We had to make the terrible decision that she be put to sleep, rather than the operation-with-possible-but-unlikely-recovery option: the troubles would only have returned in short time, and that decision would have been more to save ourselves from sadness than been best for her.

'She was a beautiful dog, so trusting and placid and utterly devoted to home and us, and we are happy we were able to give her a happy life for the last few years. We'll miss her terribly. There were many tears in this house yesterday, and they're not far away today. It's amazing how much love and connection one can feel for a dog. They're family, of course, and tug at the heart every bit as much as any child. Life goes on, but it's never quite the same.'

I wrote back as best I could. 'Always the hardest day and time. But you tell yourself they'd love you for doing the right thing, for stopping the pain and discomfort they don't really understand, for looking after them till the very end.'

When Grahame replied, he summed up how we all feel at these times.

'The extent of our love and affection is now mirrored by the depth of our distress. Sometimes a man feels like a raw and vulnerable child, and this is one of those times.'

GRAHAME AND FI'S OTHER DOG, Milo, whose sight had deteriorated in recent years, died in April 2019. Fi had taken him to Dunedin to have a troublesome ear treated, and Milo's little heart simply stopped while he was under anaesthetic.

'He went off unknowing, in a deep and painless sleep,' Grahame wrote in an email later that day. 'So there's comfort in that. A hard drive back from Dunedin for Fi, I'm afraid, and a hopelessly tearful greeting here at home.

'Life goes on. It's a bastard. But it's extraordinary too, and Milo Sydney added so much joy to ours. Farewell, our brave wee boy. We'll miss you so much.'

It seemed too tough—two dogs dying within a few

years—and I tried not to dwell on how bereft Grahame and Fi would be feeling. A month later, I sent Grahame an email, just to let him know I'd been thinking of them a great deal. Grahame replied that Milo's ashes were now in a small box on the sideboard and Fi kept a candle lit beside it.

'Such sentimental gestures, we both know,' said Grahame. 'But I refuse to cringe. It feels right, and I repeat my regulation "Good sleep, wee man" every night as I pass it and turn off the last light. It gives me some comfort.

'We intend burying Gyp and Milo's ashes together here at home, with a new tree nearby. I'm having a small plaque made. I still tear up easily. Hopeless old bastard . . . It's a quieter house, noticeably so, even though Milo scarcely uttered a sound in his mature years. But presence has sound, the sound of company, and you know too well when it's gone.'

WHEN THE FIRST BAD NEWS came from the vet about Lola, Jeremy's greying Border collie–Lab cross, all these things came into play. I'd see Jeremy most weeks at the dog park, when he'd arrive with Lola and a friend's dog, Lucy, another lithe and shiny collie–Lab. Lola always looked great, trembling with excitement each time Jeremy readied to casually catapult the ball with a thrower, while we stood around and set the world to rights. She'd slowed down a touch, and Jeremy sometimes had to give her a head start in the race against Lucy to the ball or cheat a little by lobbing it crookedly in Lola's direction. But the joy was the same to her. It was all about the game.

So, when Jeremy texted me in late September 2017 and said Lola wasn't well, that they'd been to the vet and had an X-ray and found some lumps in her stomach, I was a bit bemused. And when he added that 'she might be fucked', I thought his assessment must be wildly exaggerated because she looked far more fine than fucked.

The next week at the park, Lola seemed normal, despite her flanks having been shaved where she'd had the X-ray and ultrasound. She trotted around, snaffled the ball off Lucy and had the normal sparkle in her eyes.

And again, when Jeremy mentioned she might have only a month or two, it was hard to reconcile with how she appeared, and I stupidly continued to pretend it wasn't likely.

Jeremy spoke of how they could do surgery and chemotherapy, but that would mean weeks of recovery and discomfort for Lola. It would only be buying her a bit of time, he said, and what was the point if she spent that time feeling awful? So, given she wasn't in pain, the greater kindness was to do nothing invasive or intravenous and let Lola enjoy the days she still had. At twelve, she deserved that, he figured.

The decline was quick. As quick as Jeremy had suggested,

but far faster than the rest of us foresaw. One day in early October, Matthew arrived at the park and pulled me aside. 'Hey, you know Jeremy probably better than anyone,' he said. 'What's going on with Lola?'

The previous morning, he'd seen Jeremy, and Lola hadn't been able to walk and seemed incontinent, and Jeremy had to carry her back to the car and was obviously extremely upset. I texted Jeremy and he said, yeah, they'd thought Lola was about finished, but she'd perked up a bit and they now reckoned maybe she'd just reacted badly to some medicine she'd been given at the weekend. While her legs were 'a bit wonky', he hoped they'd be at the dog park on Friday morning.

When they didn't arrive at the normal time on Friday, I figured Lola probably wasn't up to it that morning.

But then we saw Jeremy coming down the path, cradling Lola in his arms, and setting her down by the big pōhutukawa on the park's top level. So we all trooped up to greet them, and you could see Lola was struggling, her front right leg not working properly, though she still wanted to chase the ball and snatch it from Lucy. We took turns cuddling her and she lapped it up, wagging her tail, with her eyes still bright above a muzzle of grey. Lara's wonderful young daughter, Scarlett, knelt beside her and whispered sweet nothings of love and affection, while Jeremy bravely tried to talk of politics and music, like normal. But it was pointless and we never even got on to rugby, despite the All Blacks playing the Springboks that weekend.

Finally, Jeremy said he had to go. He picked Lola up, and we all had a final stroke of her head and murmured 'good girl', while Jeremy felt the weight in his arms and the pull on his heart and did his best not to cry. He said he hoped Lola would be back at the park again, but we all knew it might not happen and this would probably be the last time. And if it was, then it was sweet and fitting and all that, Lola having a happy time in one of her favourite places.

Jeremy carried Lola back up the path, while we followed in sombre procession, and he got me to reach into his jeans pocket to get the keys and open the car door, so he could place Lola on the back seat. Lucy hopped in the back and we watched as they drove off to Jeremy's work, where the dogs would curl up and keep each other company, and Jeremy would keep a constant watch on Lola, wondering how long it would be, how long before they had to make the utterly unenviable but inevitable decision.

Their vet had always told them, 'You'll know when the time is right.' And while this seems a professional cop-out in many ways, a dereliction of guidance, it probably makes as much sense as anything in a world muddied by emotions regarding mortality. There was always going to be a line which, when breached, would make that decision clear, a line between comfort and suffering, between untroubled existence and pointless endurance. Lola hovered just above that line for days, like a seabird skimming wave tips.

When I checked in with Jeremy after the weekend and asked how Lola was, he texted, 'Up and down, hanging in there. Just been to park in Petone, and the will is strong. Still eating well.'

But, at lunchtime the next day, I got a message from him. 'Has gone all floppy in her back legs. Unless she rallies tonight, I think we will let her go tomorrow.' Then he mentioned she was at the shop where he worked 'if you want to come and say goodbye'.

So I raced down to Slow Boat Records and Jeremy ushered me into the back room, and there was Lola, lying on her side on a mattress. She lifted her head, though her tail seemed beyond wagging, but she was pretty alert and wolfed down the Garage Project dog treats I'd stashed in my pocket. Jeremy stood at the door with watery eyes and said it didn't seem like twelve years since they'd brought Lola home as a puppy. They'd got her from a pet shop in Tawa. She was part of a litter, but he couldn't remember how they'd chosen her. But often that's how it is: we don't choose them; they seem to choose us. It happens in an instant, a mix of serendipity and circumstance. She'd been so tiny.

As he stood there, Jeremy lamented—as we all do in such tender and tearful moments—that dogs just don't live long enough and how unfair it was. Jeremy and his partner, Carlena, had been together for 20 years, so Lola had been a part of their family for much of that, and just about all the time they'd lived in their current house in Petone. And when we say, 'part of their family', what we really mean is, she'd been a large part of their every day, their routine, their activities, their thinking and their emotions.

Lola's coat was still so shiny, but for the first time I thought her eyes seemed a little cloudy, their sparkle dimmed and distant. I gave her a last cuddle and whispered in her ear, and figured I wouldn't see her again.

But the next morning I texted, and Jeremy said she was quite bright, although he knew it was a brief remission. 'Vet coming tomorrow arvo,' he added.

I had to go into town, so I asked if they wanted another visit.

'Totally,' Jeremy replied.

When I arrived, they'd just got back from a drive around Wellington's south coast. They'd stopped at Lyall Bay, where surfers lolled like seals and wet dogs scampered after sticks, and Jeremy had carried Lola down to the beach where they'd sat on the sand in the sun. Then, they'd continued westwards around Cook Strait's shoreline, and when they headed back up through Brooklyn, near the dog park, Lola lifted her head in expectation. Even at their lowest, dogs still know all the usual smells and stops.

In the back of Slow Boat, Jeremy made us cups of tea, but he never drank his. His mind was elsewhere, as he played host to a stream of visitors including Lara and Scarlett who arrived to say their last goodbyes to Lola. He knew that within a day he'd be doing the same. Carlena had rung the vet to ask them to come to their home the next day, Friday, but she hadn't been able to do it—couldn't get the words out—so Jeremy had to finish the conversation and make the arrangements.

On Friday, Lola stayed home with Carlena while Jeremy went to work. Barbro popped in to see him at the shop and said he 'looked so sad and vulnerable'. Animals do that to you—they rip you open for everyone to see what's beneath the veneer and requisite bravado. But Jeremy made a good fist of hiding it, doing his fortnightly music slot with Kathryn Ryan on RNZ National without a hint of what was coming that afternoon.

Shortly afterwards, he texted me. 'Lola very dozy today. It's the right time.'

Earlier in the day, Carlena had taken Lola and her best dog buddy, Lucy, for a drive to their local delicatessen, On Trays, where the wonderful Steven Scheckter fed Lola slices of meat (he later came round to drop off a parcel of meat and cheese for Jeremy and Carlena) then to Zany Zeus where Lola had an ice cream.

After Jeremy came home, the vet arrived, and they just sat on the sofa and Lola lay her head on Jeremy's lap. She was pretty much out to it by then, so there was no flicker of resistance when the vet slid the needle under her fur.

The vet had warned that Lucy might not want to stick around for what was going to happen, but she wouldn't be shifted from the couch.

When it was over, Jeremy carried Lola outside to the vet's car to be taken for cremation, the way her body drooped heavy in his arms reinforcing the finality of it all, a piteous coda to their time together.

We were away in the South Island and I was driving when my phone pinged, so Nikki read out Jeremy's text. 'She's gone. Very hard, very sad, but she's at peace now. Thank you.'

And what do you say? Nothing that makes a difference, nothing that truly helps, other than letting the person know you care a lot. Communications at such times are inevitably full of worn-out phrases of empathy, barely better than the banalities filling the cards you find on supermarket stands, which span life's occasions: storks and popping champagne corks for newborn babies, the gilt-fringed excitement of twenty-firsts, the raunchy nonsense for those turning 40, the surprising market for those reaching 100 and then, finally, mournful sympathy cards. Some hokey old saw, some strained sentence that can never bridge the abyss between what you truly feel and what the recipient needs to hear. Some half-baked tosh that's neither truly wise nor adequately comforting. For something that happens so often, and to all of us, there sometimes just don't seem enough words.

You search for something that might provide meaning or a second of succour, and all that comes out is a dismal Hallmark verse, some saccharine sentimentality. You blurt bland things about them having 'wonderful memories', when all the person wants is more of having their dog right there, not remembering them. But maybe it's not the words that are of any real relevance. Maybe it is, after all, the thought that counts.

Jeremy used to thank me for coming to see Lola, but visiting was just a sign that I had a small idea of what he was going through, and that I realised, like we all do, that we'll go through the same thing, eventually. Like I say, that's the deal. That's the miserable contract you sign when you first lift that puppy and cradle it in the car on your way home. It's the most unbearable pact, but one you never refuse.

I mentioned this once to Barbro, after seeing a short video doing the rounds online about a guy taking his aging dog to their favourite places on one last road trip together. It was a bit mawkish, but quite beautiful, and it reinforced how the heavy-hearted last days with any pet are the heavy price we pay for the joy of having them in our life.

'Yes, but is the price not worth it?' Barbro replied.

For some, it isn't. When friends lost their pup to possum poison they'd laid on their property, they made a deliberate decision not to get another dog in spite of the fact they would have loved one. The risk of another such heartbreak was just too much for them.

Matthew said that after his last dog, a German shepherd called Schultz, died it took him five years to feel like he could get another one—and that's when Louis came along. Matthew had been through so much with Schultz, during tough times in his life. And in those circumstances, replacing your dog hastily can seem like a rejection of all you experienced together, can seem to nullify all that was and all that it meant.

Not long ago, Nikki met our friend Tara, who'd had a gorgeous big Rottweiler called Kiwa. When we first started going to Tawatawa dog park, Kiwa was one of the regulars, his giant head pressing into your thighs for a tickle, your trousers slicked with silvery slobber afterwards, as if a host of snails had passed by. Kiwa gradually got slower, the aging and decline always seeming more obvious in big dogs, and he'd died about a year ago.

When Nikki saw Tara, he was with his children, walking along Wellington's south coast towards Red Rocks and the seal colony, a popular route we often used to meet him and Kiwa along. Tara was cradling a small box containing some of Kiwa's ashes. He'd been going around Kiwa's favourite places, scattering small amounts, remembering all the happy times and walks. Scattering ashes is a fraught business in Wellington, especially along Cook Strait, and Tara had been waiting for a calm day, a perfect morning like this, unsullied by squalls. It so happened that it was

11 November, Armistice Day, so Tara had figured he'd scatter them at 11 a.m. He was also carrying a walking stick with Kiwa's name and the date he died carved into it. Tara had drilled a small hole in the bottom, inserted some ashes and plugged it, so that wherever he walked in the future Kiwa went with him. It wasn't the time to ask whether he was going to get a new dog.

IN SOME WAYS, MEASURING THE appropriate period of bereavement before getting a new dog is akin to calculating how long you should wait between the death of a spouse and starting a new relationship or remarrying.

George always had a straightforward view of these things, and a bugger-what-anyone-else-thinks attitude. In late 2017, his devoted tubby foxie, Tonto, died. Tonto had just got slower and quieter, then gradually slipped away. He was sixteen, and George had owned him for about half of that, after rescuing him from the city pound. In that time, they'd been inseparable, Tonto barely letting George out of his sight and barking madly whenever it happened.

After Tonto died, George mulled over what would be the correct length of time before looking for another dog, and figured it would be months. But before long he started casting around, thinking, *What the hell. Maybe there's another dog out there who needs a home.*

After about five weeks—'Not a very gracious amount

of time,' George admitted—he saw an ad posted on Trade Me by someone looking to rehome Sumo. He was a ten-year-old foxie-something from an Auckland family whose circumstances had changed. George wrote back saying, yes, he'd take Sumo, but then discovered the cost of relocating the small dog south was prohibitive. So the family said, 'We'll meet you halfway. See you in Taupō.'

And since then, Sumo has been George's shadow, slipping into the well-worn steps trodden by Tonto. 'He's very needy,' complains George, but you sense he actually loves that about Sumo.

When Sumo made his first appearance at the dog park, he started quietly as all the other dogs crowded around for an inspection. But any shyness lasted mere minutes. Before long, as befits stroppy foxies, he was into it— latching on to the ball-thrower John had, which was much more interesting to him than the tennis ball it flung, and barking relentlessly if it was out of reach. When I went to pick up Cooper's stick, Sumo lunged at it but missed badly, his teeth instead grabbing my bicep, leaving two lines that matched the shape of his jaws, which were later coloured in by a sickly yellow-and-mauve bruise.

'I was actually trying to get him to go for your throat,' George laughed.

Sumo's aim hadn't been too far off the mark.

George had always talked about one of his previous dogs, Aro. As Sumo made new friends and took the place of Tonto in George's life, I reminded him of something he'd once admitted to me in idle reminiscing about how when Aro died it broke his heart. 'It ripped a big part out of me. And I won't get it back,' he'd told me.

George took his eyes off Sumo briefly, and looked at me. 'They all break my heart,' he replied.

So who knows when is the right time to replace your dog. Jeremy and Carlena didn't know when it would feel right to bring another pup home into the space that was so much Lola's.

Barbro, much braver than me, raised the issue with Jeremy a few weeks after Lola died.

'Maybe in the New Year,' Jeremy said. 'I think it's probably inevitable.'

Carlena volunteered at the SPCA and was thus exposed to many unfortunate cases with longing eyes.

From the outside, it was easy to think, *Wouldn't you want to fill that enormous hole in your life as soon as possible?* But when you say that, you realise how inane it is.

There may be other things you want to do in life that are now available to you. There might not be the right dog. You might want to hold on to your old dog's memory just a little bit longer. There's no 'right' time to get another dog. I guess you just know when the time is right. Just like you do at the other end of their life.

ONE SPRING WEEKEND, CERI INVITED a group of regular park-goers to her place for a pot-luck dinner. Several times during the night, various people mentioned how lovely it was that such friendships had been born at the dog park, and how lucky it was we'd all got to know each other. But I hinted at—then sort of checked myself—the idea that this good fortune would possibly last only as long as our dogs' lives.

When your dog dies and you no longer visit the park of a morning, do the friendships survive? Many will, but in what form? Occasional meetings on city pavements or at jostling weekend vegetable markets? Take Sarah and her wee son Ethan—after their dog, Bozley, died, we lost contact with them. The dog park was too hard to cope with for Sarah when the void left by Bozley remained unfilled.

I look at our dog park community and think how phenomenally lucky I've been to meet such a fabulous circle of people, and I marvel at how close we've become. However, increasingly, I also realise that I'll probably lose some of that before long. Hamish is struggling a bit. Harry is getting on, getting portlier, getting slower. Lola has gone. Cooper is coming up ten. Muzzles are getting greyer, top speeds when sprinting across glorious open spaces are dropping. Soon, the park will change. And then what?

I'll miss terribly all the ones who will no longer come. And I choose to ignore the thought of when that will be me, of one day not having a reason to join the others at Tanera of a morning.

In a way, it's no different to a lot of friendships in life—the ones we have at school or university or various workplaces or in the towns we live. You move on, you lose contact, you might intermittently reconnect. In some ways, though, dog park friendships are different. Right from the start you know they've likely got a finite lifespan: they last as long as your dog, probably ten or twelve years. That's a long time, and in the beginning you don't really consider any of this. But as your friendships deepen and your dogs age, you start to think, *I might only get to see you and know your daily life for another two or three years.*

Lola's quick decline and death emphasised this, given I didn't want to lose regular contact with Jeremy. It made me realise the death of a dog changes things in so many ways, far beyond the awful physical emptiness that's left in your house and life.

In reality, I've always known it, but the older your dog gets the more you start thinking about it, and dreading what lies ahead.

SARAH WAS DIANA'S FRIEND. THEY'D met on their first day at primary school in Khandallah, when Diana and three other girls spotted Sarah sitting by herself wearing a stylish poncho and boots. All five of them had remained close mates and confidantes for over 40 years since that first schoolyard playtime.

So, when Sarah turned up at the dog park with her aging chocolate Labrador, Bozley, the introductions were easy, courtesy of Diana and Bonnie. Sarah would usually come with her terribly cute preschool son, Ethan, a wee man in gumboots who would play with his toy trucks on the dog park's paths while Bozley ambled and we chatted.

After leaving school, Sarah had travelled overseas, lived in Australia for ten years, become a vet nurse, then continued working at vet clinics when she returned to New Zealand from Melbourne. That return involved bringing back Bozley, who she'd adopted in Australia. He must have been one of the luckiest dogs in the world, to have Sarah as his owner, because Sarah's life revolved around caring for animals. She couldn't pass by a dog who appeared to be stray, would bring home all manner and classification of wounded and damaged animalia, and would stop the car to check the pouches of kangaroos killed on Australia's highways lest there was a surviving joey. No animal suffered if Sarah was close.

I learned all this at Sarah's funeral in January 2019.

When Bozley died of old age's complications, two days after Christmas in 2016, we didn't see Sarah at the park again.

When I wrote to say how sad we were about Bozley, Sarah emailed back. 'Definitely a difficult time. Have good moments and bad. Bozley was such a beautiful character and we will certainly keep hold of all our wonderful memories of him. Am sure Ethan would love to come to the park sometime to catch up with his "gumboot buddy" and throw the stick for Cooper, but it may be a while before I feel ready to go back there.'

We all understood exactly how Sarah was feeling, but imagined there would be another dog some time and their routine would be resumed. But it never happened.

In mid-2018, Sarah noticed a painful twinge in her side. What most would dismiss as a strain or symptom of aging turned out to be a horrible cancer around her liver. They always call such tumours 'aggressive'. I'm not sure if that's an official medical term, but it certainly summed up what was metastasising wildly inside Sarah. In a couple of weeks between early consultations, it grew a centimetre.

Much was tried, hopes were raised then destroyed, and Sarah got sicker, but she never accepted she was going to die, not to the last. How could you let yourself think that when you have a six-year-old son?

When Diana visited and sat with her the day before she died, Sarah didn't appear to be conscious, but the doctors had said she would be able to hear them—that was the last sense to go, evidently. So Diana and other friends spoke to her about old times and good times and good dogs, and Diana said how Sarah would be able to see Bozley. At this, Sarah squeezed Diana's hand.

Days later, the Khandallah Presbyterian Church was overflowing, spare chairs being placed down the aisles for the latecomers. It's the only funeral I know of where one of the songs was Cat Stevens' 'I Love My Dog'. It summed up Sarah in so many ways, and so many of those who spoke recalled her relationship with animals. There were dozens of photos attesting to that projected onto a screen, including several of Bozley, who looked young and handsome.

Diana and the three other girls who'd met Sarah that first day at school, just down the road from the church, all spoke then helped bear her coffin out into a strikingly blue and sunny Wellington day at the end of the service, while Rod Stewart's 'Forever Young' played. Sarah had just turned 48.

The day before, Ethan had been discussing the funeral with Diana and suggested they needed cupcakes afterwards. With dogs on them. 'And sweets,' he continued, 'because they make people happy.'

So that's what there was in the church hall, along with all sorts of other food, after the flower-laden hearse had been slowly driven away and disappeared. Cupcakes Diana had made the night before, brilliantly decorated with dog faces by her daughter, Iris, and sweets to make everyone just a bit happier, even though that was mighty difficult right then.

And as I drove home, there was one other thing that made me smile: the thought that, maybe, Sarah was walking Bozley, somewhere.

OF COURSE, SOMETIMES WE DIE before our dogs.

Bill and his dog would regularly walk through the park, sometimes stopping to chat, a welcome break in what seemed a slow struggle up the hill for him. He'd pause, wheeze and cough, phlegm erupting from his lungs, which was often deposited onto the grass beside me as we stood there. I don't know what emphysema looks or sounds like, but I'd put money on Bill having it.

When I first met Bill, he had Trixie, a lovely old retriever, and such was the similarity of their pace and laboured gait that I'd often worry one of them would collapse at the park. It nearly happened, I'm sure, because sometimes we'd find Bill sitting on the concrete base of the power pylons at the top of the path, catching what little breath he had. I'd offer him a ride home, but he always declined, insisting he'd be right in a minute or two.

So, after Trixie died, we were all a bit surprised when Bill reappeared with Rusty, a very energetic scruffy mongrel pup who was as strong as he was wilful, and always appeared likely to be too much for Bill, who told me he was 68. He seemed much older than that.

In March 2018, Bill died suddenly. As always, you find out more about people after they've gone. I knew Bill had been a carpenter, but little more. As a kid, he'd evidently been picked on and at school they told him he'd never be anything. He'd never married or had kids, and lived in the house he'd grown up in, for a long time caring for his

mother. He'd had issues with alcohol. One of his sisters apparently wanted little to do with him, scorning what he'd become or what he'd not become. Another would visit him weekly.

We'd just known him as wheezing Bill, who'd actually had two Trixies and two Rustys in his life, who he walked several times a day around Wellington's Central Park and through Brooklyn.

Whatever people thought of Bill's life, there was little doubt all of his dogs had good and loved existences, and that counts for so much more than what we often consider praiseworthy in a person's life.

When Bill died, we heard Rusty had gone to the pound, which filled us all with dread, but they'd assured Bill's sister he would be easily rehomed. And so it turned out. A few months later, his sister was in the Wairarapa and out walking near Greytown when she rounded a corner and who should bound up but Rusty, smiling and slightly slimmer. He'd been taken in by a couple over there who loved him to bits, and he was totally at home. Bill would have been thrilled.

IN JUNE 2018, I GOT an email from Jeremy. 'We have new pup. His name is Walnut, he's from SPCA, and has just lost his balls.'

Underneath was a photo of a brown puppy curled into

the middle of a blue beanbag. He almost looked like the kernel of a walnut, but that wasn't how he'd got his name. At the SPCA, he'd been called Wallace but, as Jeremy drove him around in those first few days, that didn't seem a good fit. The three-month-old pup was a bearded collie crossed with a Shar Pei—those wrinkly-faced dogs made popular by toilet roll ads. Not wanting to stray too far from the name he'd already got accustomed to at the SPCA, Jeremy figured he looked a bit like a walnut with his wrinkles and thought that sounded about right for a name.

As Jeremy had predicted, Carlena had spied Walnut during a session volunteering at the SPCA. She'd sent Jeremy a photo saying, 'This guy looks cute.' Shortly afterwards, she sent him another text. 'And his adoption has just fallen through . . .' She arrived home with him that night, and he's been theirs ever since—difficult to leave behind and impossible not to fall for.

Before long, Walnut was accompanying Jeremy to the record store, and hanging out with Carlena at her work at parliament, with the Speaker's indulgence. After his vaccinations had been done, Jeremy brought him to the park—a mildly nervous pup who was soon making friends and stealing balls. It was great to see, and great to see Jeremy with a dog again. And it was reassuring and comforting to know that things go on, from beginnings to sad ends to beginnings again.

Acknowledgements and apologies

Acknowledgements

MY MUM TAUGHT ME ABOUT kindness to animals and the joy of a dog in the family, and that's a priceless thing.

To Nik, who fell for Cooper the moment he sat on her lap as a timid puppy at the SPCA, and who means everything to him. I hope this reflects the amazing years we've all shared.

To Sharon, whose illustrations are simply perfect— we're so grateful you agreed to be part of this.

To publisher Jenny Hellen at Allen & Unwin, who has been so enthusiastic about this book ever since I nervously sent her some sample chapters. To Melanie, Leanne and Abba at Allen & Unwin, who have also helped *How to Walk a Dog* become a reality, and to editor Kimberley Davis, whose care and suggestions have made this a better book.

To Jane Clifton, Steve Braunias, Vincent O'Sullivan and Brian Turner for reading the manuscript and providing such kind comments.

To my editor at *North & South*, Virginia Larson, who's unstintingly encouraging, whatever the project.

To Jan and Briar for never making me feel it was my fault about what happened to Hobbs, and for being such good friends.

To Chris and David for being the best dog-sitters for Cooper when we have to go away. (Sorry about that time he stole your chicken sandwich, David.)

To all the vets at Island Bay who've cared for and patched up Cooper over the years—all with such affection and skill.

And to all the amazing people I've met while walking Cooper, especially those at Tanera Park—you're a special group of friends and it's such a wonderful way to begin my day.

Apologies

TO THE OWNERS OF ANY dogs Cooper might have growled at when they innocently got a bit close to his stick.

To our neighbours when Cooper won't shut up.

To the posties and courier drivers who Cooper meets at the gate, barking his head off—I know you don't believe it, but he really just wants to play.

To Deborah's dogs, Whetu and Hawk, who Cooper imperiously ignores, even when he's staying at their place. Likewise my sister's dog, Maverick.

I make these apologies on behalf of Cooper, but of course, in reality, I'm responsible. It's my fault I haven't trained him to be less snobby and more obedient, or ever got on top of his fixation with barking at the postie.

And Gary—we're really, really sorry about what happened at that Christmas party.

Author photo by Nikki Macdonald

About the author

MIKE WHITE HAS HAD DOGS most of his life, including a giveaway mongrel when he was a teenager, a puppy who was going to be drowned, and his current huntaway, Cooper, who features throughout *How to Walk a Dog*. They've been wonderful mates, loyal company and frequently disobedient. Some have broken his bones; all have broken his heart when they've gone.

White is one of New Zealand's best-known journalists and a senior writer at *North & South* magazine, where he has won more than 20 national media awards, including the Wolfson Fellowship to Cambridge University. In 2013 he wrote the bestselling true crime book *Who Killed Scott Guy?*

He lives in Wellington with his partner, Nikki, and they walk Cooper along the coast, through the bush and at the city's dog parks.